University Parks
F
O
R
D
Pitt Rivers
Natural History Museum
Wadham
Bridge of Sighs
Bodleian Library
Radcliffe Camera
All Souls
St Mary's
High St
Magdalen
Addison's Wk
Magdalen Br
Botanic Gardens
Merton Fields
Corpus Christi
Christ Church Meadow
CHERWELL
Iffley Rd

This Secret Garden

BY THE SAME AUTHOR

INTERIOR

LOOK AT IT THIS WAY

MASAI DREAMING

IN EVERY FACE I MEET

LEADING THE CHEERS

HALF IN LOVE

WHITE LIGHTNING

THE PROMISE OF HAPPINESS

THE SONG BEFORE IT IS SUNG

This Secret Garden

Oxford Revisited

Justin Cartwright

BLOOMSBURY

First published in Great Britain 2008

Endpaper map by Jeff Fisher

Bloomsbury Publishing Plc, 36 Soho Square, London W1D 3QY

ISBN 978 0 7475 7961 8

10 9 8 7 6 5 4 3 2 1

A CIP catalogue record for this book is available from the British Library

Typeset by Hewer Text UK Ltd, Edinburgh
Printed in Great Britain by Clays Limited, St Ives plc

The paper this book is printed on is certified by the © Forest Stewardship Council 1996 A.C. (FSC). It is ancient-forest friendly. The printer holds FSC chain of custody SGS-COC-2061

FSC
Mixed Sources
Product group from well-managed forests and other controlled sources

Cert no. SGS-COC-2061
www.fsc.org
© 1996 Forest Stewardship Council

Once snagged in these potent streets, once admitted to this secret garden, the initiated cannot leave. It remains a place whose friendships and mutual succour, its secret languages and codes, will go on being shared.

– Valentine Cunningham, *The History of the University of Oxford*, vol. 8

FOREWORD

[illegible] it a [illegible] [illegible] I have to admit [illegible] about the [illegible] University of Oxford. The two [illegible] inseparable in my mind.

Recently an interviewer, [illegible] towards the [illegible] Oxford [illegible] as possible. [illegible] what I am, [illegible] Oxford, but an Oxford [illegible]

Oxford is many things, [illegible] meaning well beyond its [illegible] and teaching. It stands for something deep in the Anglo-Saxon psyche — [illegible] kind of privilege, a [illegible] deep [illegible] liberalism, a respect for [illegible]

[illegible] a place. [illegible]

FOREWORD

This book is one in a series called 'The Writer and the City'. I have to admit now that it is not so much about the City of Oxford as the University of Oxford. The two are anyway inseparable in my mind.

Recently an interviewer, after being very cordial towards me in person, complained in print that I worked Oxford into my life story as quickly as possible. It is true. Oxford made me what I am, although it was not the real Oxford, but an Oxford I imagined.

Oxford is many things. But it has a symbolic meaning well beyond its buildings, gardens, rituals and teaching. It stands for something deep in the Anglo-Saxon mind – excellence, a kind of privilege, a charmed life, deep-veined liberalism, a respect for tradition.

It is also a place. This for me is the fascination of

cities, that they are both places – an accumulation of bricks and stone and architecture and landscape – and at the same time the accumulation of hopes, aspirations, intellectual effort and human striving. The fusion is what defines a particular city.

From the moment I arrived at Trinity College in the mid-sixties, I was in love with Oxford. It plumped up my dry colonial heart; I loved the first autumn term, the darkness, gowned figures on bicycles, crumpets after rugby, the pale – although not very numerous – girls, the extraordinary buildings and the water running through and around the town. I felt as though I had always known the place, or some simulacrum of it, in another or parallel life.

After I left I could hardly bear to go back: it was as if nobody else should take possession of this place that had meant so much to me, in fact formed me. I was almost embarrassed by how easily and totally I had been seduced. It took me nearly two years to get over the desolation of having to live in London.

Now I have been back and tried to understand what Oxford is, was, and might be. It's a personal account, an essay handed in late.

I

I am staring at myself in a hotel bathroom mirror. At the same time I am eating the last part of a club sandwich. My face is strangely contorted, as though I am puzzled by the act of eating or lacking sufficient teeth for the job. My brow has spots on it, clearly melanin, which in a novel I once described casually as 'the rain spots of mortality'. That was some years ago. It may be because of the jet lag – it's three in the morning – that I feel so disoriented. When I look at myself under the neon in all those mirror images multiplying promiscuously, I see something almost loathsome: a spotted, middle-aged man – more than middle-aged – with a little circlet of hair, so that I look like a prelate or an ineffectual vicar. Not that many vicars are wolfing club sandwiches in the Westin Plaza Harbour Hotel, Toronto, at three in the morning.

Other manifestations of Western culture are, I am sure, present in other rooms, although I don't hear the muffled cries of sexual pleasure or the moans of suicide or the confident roars of drunken salesmen.

Last week I was in Oxford. It was Freshers' Week. Long shadows fell on the Front Quad of Trinity, my old college; it was a perfect autumn day, when the air is loaded with moisture and the grass is faceted and the trees are drooping heavily. Outside the rooms the college had given me – evocatively decorated with a stained carpet, some Swedish not-so-modern furniture, a few old pieces that were short of a home – young febrile voices had chattered. They were gathering for the Freshers' Dinner, to be addressed by Michael Beloff, President of the college. Oxford colleges started as lodging houses or halls and the head is variously described as Master, Warden, Provost, Principal, President or, in the case of Christ Church, Dean. Each college remembers its past jealously. My rooms looked out on to two quads, Durham and Garden, completely enclosed by the chapel, the hall and various staircases. (How easily I slip into this self-congratulatory, clubby mode.) The sun was very low and the lanterns on the walls were already yellowing the stone. The windows of the chapel had become dark shards of glass. Stained glass is intended to be seen from within, from the enclosed religious space. From the outside it is usually opaque. The basin by the bedroom window was a wonderful detail, speaking eloquently of a contempt for interior design; from there I could see Garden Quad, open at one end to Trinity's glorious gardens where, in the fading light, the herbaceous border, at least a hundred yards long, was conducting a vigorous last stand against winter. There, looking out over the massed shrubs and flowers, is a bust of Cardinal Henry Newman, Trinity's most famous cleric, who left Oxford and never returned after he was ordained as a Roman Catholic Priest. Michael Beloff later suggested that one day he might well be beatified. Newman's features are thin and somewhat blank; I imagine a man who feels pity for the less spiritual. He found his time at Trinity a trial: 'I really think, if anyone should ask me what qualifications were necessary for Trinity College, I should say there was only one, drink, drink, drink.' But like almost everyone who has ever been to Oxford, he kept strong feelings for the place. As Philip Larkin puts it in his 'Poem About Oxford', 'The old place still holds us.'

The old place still holds me. Outside, the voices had an unfamiliar timbre and I realised what it was: girls' voices, Oxford prefers to call them women, but these were unmistakably girls, children, chattering brightly, chiming nervously. Only much later in the night did I hear something more familiar, the bull-calf bellow of a drunken public schoolboy. The college looked the same, but the rasping masculinity, the heavy, wet cricket jumpers, the pee in the basins – the roaring-boy chorus – had been muted. One of the funniest books in the English language is *Decline and Fall*: poor Paul Pennyfeather's treatment by the hearties now has an anthropological quality, a report on an almost lost tribe of philistines. The moment in the book I love best is the porter's sage observation: 'Like most undergraduates sent down for indecency, you will take to schoolmastering.'

Later that night I sat in the gallery of the Hall looking down. The candles were lit, the college silver beamed triumphantly, like an old person on an outing from a home for seniors. Latin grace was said under the portrait of Sir Thomas Page, the founder, before the college servants, formally dressed in dark trousers and waistcoats, moved in. Below the Adam urns that decorated the gallery, I put my head in my hands and wept. The tears were brief and strangely pleasurable, something like being moved in the cinema. What was it that moved me?

Now in Toronto, hopelessly confused, I look back on those few days and the morning after the dinner when I woke to find the quads outside the windows glowing moistly in a low October sun after a night rain. The stone flags had the colour of a Christmas ham, glazed with honey. Michael Beloff had said in his address to the freshers that they had all been chosen on merit, no matter what their background or schooling: 'At Trinity we discriminate neither in favour of nor against anyone. We believe that you are very lucky to be here and that we are very lucky to have you.' That week Beloff had caused some mutterings by suggesting that government get its tanks off Oxford's lawn. And this is a feature of Oxford that outsiders, and even some living within its quadrangles and enclosed gardens, believe, that there is something too privileged about the life. Looking down on the freshers that evening, I found it hard to imagine any comparable group of students outside Oxbridge enjoying a dinner like this, candlelit, securely framed within the perfect hall, the atmospheric pressure rising as they began to relax. And there was plenty of symbolism on view for those who knew where to look; the Jewish President of the college presiding over a Latin grace, spoken by the Anglican chaplain, the portraits of the great and the good suggesting, semaphoring, a kind of ease with history and tradition, even the Christianity that motivated the founder comfortably absorbed into a sort of liberal and urbane tolerance; a sense – not peculiarly Oxonian but always present there – that history, religion, art, science and ethics are all the servants of a liberal society, not its master; the sense that values are a human creation, not some discoverable text. I remembered the sixties when Tariq Ali led a march down to the Law Library, about to be opened by Harold Wilson, and Oxford protested; it was, I felt, a protest conducted ironically. Whatever social historians say now, the sixties student rebellion passed over Oxford at a very high altitude, not because Oxford was smug, but because the issues at stake were, in that comfortable, alert world, well understood and thoroughly debated. The dons themselves were often more radical than their students. And this is one of the things about Oxford that outsiders find infuriating, that it teaches scepticism and self-deprecation not out of humility but out of a sense of superiority, something which D.H. Lawrence recognised clearly. Tariq Ali, I came to think, was tolerated out of a kind of condescension, almost as though Oxford could easily incorporate some campus revolutionary. Indeed Tariq himself may have been complicit.

Robertson Davies, the Canadian novelist, said: 'The greatest gift Oxford gives its sons is a genial irreverence towards learning. And from this irreverence, love may spring.' The view of Lord David Cecil, still functioning when I was up (as we say), that 'as a critic I would not advise the study of any work after 1914' is an even more extreme example of an identifiable Oxford tendency to shy away from any form of bandwagon, social or academic. In Cecil's case, admittedly, it was difficult to separate the contrarian from the old-fashioned reactionary.

Michael Beloff told the freshers that, while the college had a proper concern for their pastoral care, it expected high standards of application and behaviour: 'It is not necessary to get drunk *every* night,' he said. (I have the transcript of the speech, and he has underlined *every*.) And I wondered if this wasn't in some sense also Oxonian, as these children were unashamedly being served wine from the college's stocks. Underneath Oxford are thousands and thousands of bottles of wine, laid down by committees of interested dons. But also underneath Oxford, stretching right under Broad Street, are millions of books, not merely books designed to aid the student in passing a degree, but Islamic and Hebraic collections, political papers, ephemera, a Shakespeare First Folio, Cranmer's Bible, Kafka's manuscripts and much, much more, a richness almost beyond comprehension. And above ground, Duke Humfrey's Library, built in 1488, is one of the most beautiful libraries in the world and retains much of the original shelving and book storage of its early days. It was in Duke Humfrey's that I worked on my thesis forty years ago. And now, during Freshers' Week, I applied to the Bodleian again and was delighted, flattered, to find I was still on record and could be issued with a card: my new card holds a slightly washed-out, even ghostly, image of me looking just like my father.

And it is this self I am facing in a Canadian mirror, the older self, setting out on the downhill slope of life.

Last week in Oxford I made a lightning tour of the town, photographing everything I could, because I was finding it difficult to distinguish between my memories of Oxford and what I saw now.

And as I look in the mirror at what I have become, I try to recall every picture I took. I can remember the small boys of Magdalen College School at rugby practice on Merton Fields most clearly; they are wearing scarlet rugby jerseys and being supervised by a beefy, enthusiastic young man. Behind them is the tower of Merton College and off to the west the spire of Christ Church Cathedral, soaring, but still firmly moored. These boys have the pale, unformed legs of ten- and eleven-year-olds. They are playing rugby in one of the most beautiful places in England: on the one side the ancient college walls and spires and gateways; on another the Isis in the autumn sunshine flashing through trees, and, sweeping off in a large parabola, Christ Church Meadow, whose cows, perfectly placed, some lying down, some standing, chew the cud, unaware, of course, that they are part of a highly artificial tableau, a landscape so composed, so close to perfection, that for the second time in a few days I find myself struggling with self-regarding tears.

Oxford is the city of youth, but it is also the city of those who stayed on, the people Larkin described as the *arselickers*. That day I saw from the tower of St Mary the Virgin – the finest view of Oxford – the great and the good processing towards All Souls from the ceremony of installing the new Vice Chancellor, Dr John Hood, who believed he had the task of reforming the university. It is hard to be precise what reform means at Oxford, but almost everyone always thinks that it is overdue. Those in the procession were universally grey, with that slightly abstracted, childlike look I have come to associate with academics, the clever boys and girls who never quite grow up. Led by proctors in bowler hats, carrying, if I remember, staves of office, they marched past the Radcliffe Camera, the most extravagant building in Oxford, towards All Souls, their gowns fluttering and flashing like the underwings of exotic birds exposed in flight. From up on the tower I could see them reappear in the wonderful Hawksmoor-designed North Quad of All Souls and mill about underneath Christopher Wren's huge sundial before entering the Codrington Library, a place where the air is so refined and the access so limited as to make it the Potala Palace of Oxford. Undergraduates and researchers may use the library, but they must work in a separate, smaller room, while the vast main reading room is reserved for fellows and visiting fellows of All Souls. In there the middle-aged and the elderly who make up Oxford's governing body – itself under threat from reforms – could revivify themselves with deep draughts, great lungfuls of this fine air, and remind themselves that this is no ordinary university. And they could drink the college's antique wine brought up from the cellars by aged servants. Or so I imagined.

And that day I passed along behind the Botanical Gardens to Magdalen and photographed a branch of mountain ash in bright berry against the stone of a Gothic window. The stone in Oxford is often described, I have found, as grey, but in fact it is mostly a sort of washed-out russet, like the skin of an obsolete apple, the sort of apple that finds its way to my local farmers' market. Much of Oxford is built of limestone from Headington, where the first quarry was dug in 1396. Most notably, New College, the Divinity School, All Souls and Christ Church were built with it. At one time ten colleges owned their own quarries. Six thousand, one hundred and forty wagonloads were needed for All Souls alone. The walk through Christ Church Meadow is the old wagon track, laid out especially from Headington. But by the middle of the eighteenth century it was discovered that Headington limestone eroded badly, and quarrying in Headington wound down. It's this erosion, which has to be patched up all the time, that leaves some Oxford buildings looking like frayed linen that has been through the wash too often. Now the stone used is Clipsham, Portland, Ironstone, Cotswold, Lincolnshire and Bath.

Of course, I found it all deeply affecting, that stone itself could be so old it needed repair; for someone from South Africa, this stone seemed to speak, even sing, of a kind of seriousness and a disregard for time. People from the newer worlds don't so much have no history as no understanding of how brief historical time has been. Stonemasonry of the old sort – of the Jude Fawley (the stonemason hero of *Jude the Obscure*) sort – demanded decades, even generations, to complete and to me it seemed like an act of faith. One of the qualities of Oxford even now is a palpable sense of establishment, of hewn stone and stone walkways and cobbled quadrangles; it's an accumulation of labour – which in a sense is what all cities are – but in Oxford the purpose of that labour is poignantly visible in the buildings: they are, as in Venice, a kind of art that transcends craft because it speaks directly to the human spirit. As I read this last sentence back, I make no apology; my twenty-year-old self and my middle-aged self are one on this (although not much else): cities are, or can be, man's supreme art form.

Just before his eightieth birthday my friend Geza Vermes, retired Professor of Jewish Studies, described to me his first sight of St Giles' when he arrived in England stateless and jobless, forty-five years ago: 'I thought I had woken up in heaven.' There is a psychological disorder known as Jerusalem syndrome, and I believe that there is something similar in Oxford, a sort of ecstatic state that true believers enter. In Jerusalem people run around dressed as Jesus Christ or as prophets and have visions on the Mount of Olives, or they see the dead rising outside the Essene Gate. In Oxford they wear gowns and ride bicycles with baskets on the front of them, and remember the day they saw a vision of Isaiah Berlin sailing down the High.

The last of the club sandwich is in sight. It has congealed so that the bacon and the white bread have fused in some way. But still I eat on, because it's three in the morning and I am thinking about the passage of time, something no sane person should ponder at this hour. There I am in the mirror, disappearing in an arc of sadly distorted images, when it comes to me: it's no great insight, but I see that Oxford, for all its ancient and fraying stone, for all its processions of grey-haired men and women, for all its millions of books, is in essence a city of youth: the books, the dons, the buildings are sets and props against which youth parades itself. For three or four years the young pass through Oxford, a changing cast, but unchanging in their youth. I remember what Edmund Burke wrote: 'The arrogance of age must submit to be taught by youth.' There is a tension in Oxford, a poignancy like that of a phrase of music or a fragment of poem, a poignancy that can pierce very deep. At this moment, as I survey myself in a mirror, it has the force of a mystic revelation.

Later I read what Isaiah Berlin wrote to Adam von Trott after he, Adam, had left Oxford: 'This place is going to be a mausoleum next year, the constants all there, the variables all gone.' Ten years later, von Trott was hanged by Hitler for his part in the Bomb Plot of 20 July 1944.

2

There are many Oxfords. When I try to dig down to the essence of Oxford, my Oxford at least, I come to Isaiah Berlin. When Berlin died in 1997, William Waldegrave said, 'If you had asked me to show you what I meant by the ideal of Englishness, I would have taken you to see a Latvian, Jewish, German, Italian mixture of all the cultures of Europe. I would have taken you to see Isaiah Berlin.'

One of the things that has struck me all my adult life is the extraordinary amount of energy that has been wasted on the hope that life has meaning. Berlin understood with penetrating clarity that people who seek an all-embracing theory in religion and philosophy are deluded. He started his career as a philosopher, but could not agree with the logical positivists like A.J. Ayer, who had been deeply affected by the new philosophy of Vienna and by Wittgenstein, that all meaningful statements were either analytic or empirical. Metaphysical statements were entirely meaningless. Berlin saw early that logical positivism was striving to make itself into a sort of science, and turned away from it. Determinism was another of his bugbears: determinism suggested that every event has a cause, which could usefully be understood. A faith in determinism implied a belief that philosophy could yield in a scientific fashion a complete explanation of everything that happens, an idea which Berlin rejected. His friend and colleague, J.L. Austin, said to him one day, 'They all *talk* about determinism and *say* they believe in it, but I have never met a determinist in my life, I mean a man who really did believe in it as you and I believe that men are mortal. Have you?' Berlin was very conscious that philosophy had detached itself from common sense. Heavily under the influence of Wittgenstein, and temperamentally sceptical, Oxford philosophers were eager to get to the nub of the nature of knowledge through language. They would alight on a sentence or even a single word in anything vaguely metaphysical and ask what the speaker meant by that word. The tradition lives on: Oxford philosophy is more often about the sense of words and the meaning of claims and statements than about the life-enhancing properties of philosophy, which sometimes comes as a surprise to neophyte undergraduates. Berlin tired quickly of philosophy. It was self-evident, he said, that one *can* meaningfully discuss concepts like freedom, ethics, imagination and art. He gave as an example music, which can have an undeniably powerful effect on mood and sensibility, even if it has no 'meaning' of itself. At the other extreme, the more spiritual idea of philosophy he found even more repellent, the kind of nonsense that led to war, the idea that *Geist* existed and was, like a wagon train on the prairies, rolling ever onwards to a quasi-religious destination where a resolution would take place. He was fond of a quote of Bishop Butler, the eighteenth-century divine: 'Things and actions are what they are, and the consequences of them will be what they will be: why then should we desire to be deceived?' Berlin decided that the history of ideas would be his field of study, rather than the doomed attempt to find the incorrigible proposition.

And this, I came to believe, is the ethos of Oxford: there is no overarching theory, there is no God, there is no life after death, there are no moral precepts that exist outside society or history and there is no libretto or script for life. Instead we live life as we can and make of it what we can, and we behave decently and ethically because that is the sensible, and indeed the only, way to live. What we have to fall back on is our sense that 'Everything is what it is: liberty is liberty, not equality or fairness or justice or culture, or human happiness or a quiet conscience. If the liberty of myself or my class or nation depends on the misery of a number of other human beings, the system which promotes this is unjust and immoral.'

Two Concepts of Liberty, Berlin's astonishing re-evaluation of freedom, had reached us in Johannesburg where I was studying politics (as well as French, English and philosophy). It was a turbulent time, with Mandela recently sentenced to life in prison and an inchoate struggle developing between the liberals and the determinists in the university. There was plenty of glamorous talk of Trotskyites and Stalinists, and even some real Communists among us, two of whom are now high in the ANC government. I once went out with some friends, all of us drunk, of course, to try to destroy an electrical pylon; it wasn't easy with an empty brandy bottle and a tyre iron and we soon gave up, but it was symptomatic of my youthful political stance: absolute repudiation of the tyranny of the government, but a deep suspicion of what was on offer as an alternative. So when I read *Two Concepts of Liberty*, it chimed immediately: there are no quasi-scientific or religious solutions to the problems of society; true freedom is what Berlin called 'freedom from', negative freedom, which was freedom from injustice and oppression. That excluded any Marxist blueprint into which individuals were supposed to subsume themselves in order to achieve 'freedom to'. Berlin was deeply suspicious of the idea that true freedom could be achieved only in this way, by serving the state or the party, and he was vehemently opposed to the idea that we are living with a false consciousness, which only the leaders of a society or a party can correct.

It all seemed so clear, suddenly so obvious to me. Typically, when Berlin was about to deliver his Inaugural Lecture as Chichele Professor on 31 October 1958, he feared that what he was about to say would be regarded as 'sonorous platitudes'. Hugh Trevor-Roper, in fact, noted that the lectures were 'less gay than I had hoped'. These sonorous platitudes developed over the years into the most powerful justification of liberalism in the twentieth century. It strikes me as being of the utmost importance to understand what Berlin was saying: for a start he was sceptical of the idea, popular since Aristotle, that we are all political animals. Instead, he said, politics is the inescapable element of human affairs, because human goals are often in conflict. Politics is not an emancipating activity, merely a necessary one.

I am reminded of this in Toronto, sharing a platform with Gillian Slovo, the writer and daughter of Joe Slovo and Ruth First, ANC activists. She said, in response to a question from the audience, 'It's all politics,' in the knowing way of true believers. The audience nodded and chuckled. I wondered how many knew that they were listening to the daughter of a KGB-funded Communist. Back in Johannesburg, I had come to see that what was missing in South Africa was exactly that, politics: politics in the sense that Berlin articulates it, the free and open play of ideas in conflict, toleration, free discussion, respect for the opinion of others. I think it is true to say that the present government of South Africa has no instinctive feeling for these ideas; it is still prisoner to the myth of the movement and the faith of determinism.

As Bishop Butler said, why should we desire to be deceived? I don't know why so many people appear to want to be deceived, nor do I know why they believe in the irrational and in the idea that history is going somewhere. Marcel Mauss, the French ethnographer, wrote that he and his colleagues in France could not have imagined that a whole people could have fallen prey to Hitler's delusions. Up until then the idea that the world was freeing itself from delusion prevailed in the Sorbonne where Mauss taught. Mauss killed himself in 1950. I mention this in conjunction with Isaiah Berlin because Berlin was between 1930 and 1933 a close friend of Adam von Trott zu Solz, a German Rhodes Scholar at Balliol. Von Trott came from an old Hessian family. In England he soon attracted interest and made a wide circle of friends with people as distinguished and as varied as Maurice Bowra, Goronwy Rees, Shiela Grant Duff, David Astor and the Master of Balliol, A.D. Lindsay. He had a highly developed sense of himself as a man with a higher calling, which Berlin found faintly ridiculous. Von Trott was a Hegelian, and Hegel was the intellectual begetter of the idea that we are servants of history. By this time Berlin had come to loathe German philosophy, and in particular Hegelianism, which he called 'vaporous clouds of nonsense'.

He was moving, slowly, to his much more pragmatic view of philosophy and ethics, but he was, like all his group at Oxford, still influenced by logical positivism and its attempts to reduce philosophy to a form of linguistics. As Stuart Hampshire said at the time: 'Ethics have little rational content of any kind.' Berlin saw that this kind of thing, the minute examination of the meaning of every statement, could lead to sterility. 'We cannot speak without incurring risk,' he said. He and von Trott used to stride around Addison's Walk at Magdalen talking, arguing and gossiping. In 1933, after a disappointing second-class degree, von Trott returned to Germany, to Berlin's dismay. Berlin was already very conscious of the dark nature of Hitler's plans: he was one of the few people in Oxford to have read and taken seriously *Mein Kampf*. And he and Maurice Bowra were familiar with Stefan George, the poet of a higher and mystical German nationalism, someone the Nazis tried to claim as their own when they came to power. George died just in time.

But von Trott was determined to save his country from what he saw very early as a madness. He was intensely patriotic at a time when his Oxford friends saw patriotism as bombast. He refused initially to join the Nazi Party, but practised law as a prosecutor in Hesse. In 1934 he wrote a letter to the *Manchester Guardian*, in which he said that in his experience Jews were not discriminated against in the legal process. In fact, he wrote, he had talked to some brownshirts who, although they shared their Führer's views, would never mistreat Jews. It was a turning point for Berlin. Up until then he had always seen both sides of most issues, but this changed him: von Trott's letter was absolutely wrong. Although he wrote one or two warm personal letters to von Trott, Berlin never relented. He knew that ideas can have consequences. Von Trott's friends tried to defend him: Astor to his dying day suggested that von Trott was establishing cover as he was already a member of the opposition to Hitler, even though his mother herself said that, the moment he posted the letter, he regretted it and tried to have publication stopped. One of Berlin's letters to von Trott's great friend Shiela Grant Duff is extremely severe:

> It is very well to argue that Adam had to write bogus reports in order to keep in with the Nazis

> and conceal his own true activities . . . Anyway, let it be. Let him be sent to history as a pure-hearted democrat and man of rigid principle, and not an ambitious, fascinating, self-romanticising, personally delightful and politically ambivalent figure with a passion for very high-level intrigue. The question is whether good looks, charm, patriotism, and courage are enough; I think you almost used to think they were. Do you still?

The last sentence I take to be a sly reference to her near love affair: von Trott proposed marriage to her, although he knew she was in love with Goronwy Rees. As war came closer, von Trott continued to try to use his influence in Britain and in America to prevent it. He went to Turkey, Switzerland, Sweden and Holland on various missions to drum up support for the opposition. It was a suicidally dangerous position to adopt while working for the German Foreign Office, something he was only able to do after reluctantly joining the Party. His last trip abroad was to Sweden in January 1944, where he met Willy Brandt. Later in the year he was one of those involved in the 20 July Bomb Plot, and on 24 August he was brutally hanged after a show trial, leaving a wife (who is still alive) and two daughters.

Berlin's scepticism about what he saw as von Trott's self-appointed mission in life – his 'taste for very high-level intrigue' – which led him and Maurice Bowra to warn leading figures in the US against von Trott – must have been severely tested by the nature of his death. In later years Berlin wrote a gracious memoir of von Trott in the Balliol magazine, but in private, while acknowledging his attractive qualities, he continued to think of him as deluded, and was quite vehement in his disapproval of Astor's continuing apologia. What Berlin saw was that von Trott believed in Germany's destiny; destiny was an abhorrent idea to Berlin, who thought it was at the bottom of all totalitarianism. Having now read the correspondence and many of Berlin's books, I believe that very early on, because of his wide reading and mastery of the relevant European languages, Berlin had an extraordinarily acute idea of how it was that Germany was deluded by Hitler.

When news of von Trott's execution reached Oxford, the Rhodes Trust discussed how they should record his death in their bulletins. At first it was suggested that he should be listed as a casualty of war, but the decision was put off until after the war. Grave suspicions – some of them undoubtedly originating with Berlin – that von Trott was at the very least an ambivalent figure failed to go away. This story has an added and awful poignancy: von Trott wrote to Christabel Bielenberg in 1944, not long before his death:

> I owe more to Oxford than I can say, but it's a strange thing, when I decided to come back to Germany in 1933, I would have thought I did exactly what most of my Oxford friends would have done if they were faced with a Hitler in their own country. Yet the very fact that I did come back aroused, I think, nothing but distrust – damaging distrust. I sometimes wonder how many friends I have there now – I mean real friends.

Maurice Bowra wrote on hearing of his death, 'That's one Nazi who was hanged.' Yet in his memoirs published in 1966, he recanted, saying his rejection of von Trott had caused him 'much unhappy searching of heart'; he was, he says, completely wrong to have ordered von Trott out of his house in 1939, believing that the Gestapo would never have allowed him to speak so freely. Bowra wrote to Felix Frankfurter, FDR's friend and adviser, in America warning him against von Trott, who was proposing a visit to Washington. About the hanging, he later wrote, 'I was wrong. I saw how mistaken I had been, and my rejection of him remains one of my bitterest regrets.' (When I read this, I thought, pedantically, that it should have been 'most bitter regrets'.)

Astor never wavered in his loyalty to von Trott and not long before his death in 2001, he wrote, with Shiela Grant Duff, a defence of his friend. Now that Shiela Grant Duff is dead, there is a minor scandal about the letters von Trott wrote to her; von Trott's family would like, at the least, copies returned, as they returned her letters to von Trott many years ago. The friendship between Shiela Grant Duff and von Trott was disputatious and complicated by his intense feelings for her. I have read those of these letters that have been published, and the originals of von Trott's letters to Berlin in the Bodleian Library: his English is impeccable, just a little stilted at times, and his handwriting is astonishing, almost calligraphy. I find his feelings for Oxford and his Oxford friends deeply moving, and reading the letters themselves intensifies this sense. I am aware, however, of a tendency to appropriate the emotions of others for myself.

The relationship between von Trott and Berlin points to aspects of Oxford that I recognise. The first, and probably the most obvious, is the very high regard for Oxford in the world at large. Whatever its detractors say about Oxford's failings, it is almost universally seen as unique. The uniqueness is because it is woven into the culture of the English-speaking world. In one of my books a character describes Oxford as 'the Lourdes of Englishness'. As a South African it seemed to me before I got there that Oxford might well work a miracle on me, transforming me into something else. And it did, in my mind at least. At Oxford I felt for the first time in my life that I was in the right place. When Geza Vermes told me that he thought he had wound up in heaven, it occurred to me that you need to come from somewhere else to appreciate Oxford fully. No doubt if you come from Eton or Winchester, you arrive at Oxford feeling that the furniture has just been moved. But for Berlin, for von Trott – as well as for me – I think it's true to say that Oxford appeared to be a distillation, an accumulation, of what is important in human endeavour in general, but in the Anglophone world in particular. Von Trott's letters are shot through with his fervent desire that Germany should maintain, or regain, its good reputation in England, which he often elides with Oxford. Oxford's relative importance has declined, but its hold on the imagination is still strong. The *Evening Standard* columnist Victor Lewis-Smith recently proclaimed one of his rules, that everyone who was at Oxford would announce that fact within eleven minutes of the start of any conversation. I'm afraid it is true of me. As I have said, I hear myself insinuating it into the conversation right on cue. But it is also true that many people who didn't get in to Oxford wish they had. I loved this from another journalist, Giles Coren:

> You can always tell a person who went to a good second-rank university because within the first ten minutes of meeting you, they will say, 'You can always tell a person who went to Oxford or Cambridge because they will tell you about it within the first ten minutes of meeting you.' It's funny, it's only people who got their degree from universities at the top of

the second division, the 'A and two Bs' places that are second on everyone's UCAS list and top of nobody's, who do this.

People who were at Oxford almost invariably want their children to go there too. Take Stephen Spender's grammatically mangled entries in his diary:

> Suddenly realised that I want very much that Matthew should go to Oxford. That if it is an élite, that his friends are going there, and that if he doesn't he will be left behind by the best members of his generation . . . it is a thought that runs contrary to my principles and even my sympathies, but I realised that I thought my Oxford contemporaries as in some way superior beings. Going there made me enjoy such conversations and exchange of ideas in circumstances of easy companionship and comparative leisure with the best contemporaries of one's generation during their most formative years.

The other aspect of Oxford that many become aware of early on is that, for all its beautiful old buildings, secluded quads, and arcane practices, Oxford is a worldly place. Modern politics and journalism in Britain have, until recently, largely been fashioned in Oxford. So what is discussed at Oxford will find its way into the public domain quite quickly. The heyday of the don as adviser to government may have passed but Oxford's influence is still pervasive. In recent times you have only to look at the Butler *Inquiry into Weapons of Mass Destruction* or Michael Beloff's offensive against lowered academic standards, Gordon Brown's intervention in the Laura Spence case in 2000, when he described her rejection by Magdalen as absolutely outrageous, and, earlier but no less public, the rejection in 1985 of an honorary degree for Margaret Thatcher, to realise that Oxford and its opinions and its attitudes are still taken very seriously, perhaps disproportionately so. I have spoken to two of the dons who were behind the opposition to Mrs Thatcher. The cuts to education were their main objection. They felt that someone who could take this line with the universities could not expect to be nodded in. Professor Peter Pulzer, of All Souls, one of the more visible figures in the opposition, said at the time:

> This is not a radical university, it is not an ideologically motivated university. I think we have

> sent a message to show our very great concern, our very great worry about the way in which educational policy and educational funding are going in this country. I hope the Prime Minister and the Government and the country at large will take note.

The opposition campaign, I was told, was better organised, organisation being a traditional leftist virtue. In the event the vote against Mrs Thatcher was huge, 738 to 319. As a result she gave her papers to Cambridge, although she continued to support her old college, Somerville. There are still some in Oxford who think turning her down for an Honorary Doctorate of Civil Law was an irresponsible gesture, which gave licence to those in Westminster who like to think that Oxford is out of touch. Honorary degrees for prime ministers are more or less standard, in any event. These people fear that the same thing happened again when the dons voted down the proposed changes of 2007, which, of course, the Vice Chancellor presented as reforms.

So important is Oxford in the public mind that the call of the Oxford Union or the invitation to some grand college dinner is seldom ignored. And this seems to me the most interesting aspect of Oxford, that it is seen in the outside world as a version of the ideal community, which possesses in its very fabric something precious and universal, human qualities that the world at large cannot afford to lose. And it is the collegiate system that makes Oxford and Cambridge what they are. Both teaching and loyalty are centred on the college, and the college heads are frequently public figures. Michael Beloff in his speech to the freshers in Trinity that evening stressed that it was the college that had admitted them, and that it was the college that would care for them: 'You have come up to Oxford, but the college has chosen you.' Oxford, as a university, is less real to the undergraduates than their college. Many don't understand the relationship between college and university. But the colleges are reluctant to lose their power of decision, their control of admissions and their independent financial status, and they believe that although there should be reform and coordination, there is no need for them to surrender their independence.

For all its civilised aspect, Oxford is prone to rancour. Oxford anthologies of anecdotes are full of cruel snobbery, philistinism and vicious put-downs. There is a great deal of pettiness in everyday politics and appointments and promotion really cause the knives to be produced. A sort of witty cynicism has long been prized, including Bowra's. But as the years go by his aphorisms, for example, 'I am more dined against than dining', seem to be less and less brilliant, merely self-regarding. Although 'Buggery was invented to fill that awkward hour between evensong and cocktails' is rather brilliant, as is his description of Enid Starkie, Reader in French, arriving at a party in 'all the colours of the Rimbaud'. And I also like 'Awful shit, never met him'. The literature of Oxford dons, from Lewis Carroll to Tolkien and C.S. Lewis, suggests that a certain infantilism is admired. (Iris Murdoch is another matter.) Waugh, perhaps Oxford's greatest twentieth-century writer, with his defiant third and his abhorrence of all literary pretension, is the perennial Oxford novelist, and John Betjeman with his pass degree (a degree given to those who went through the motions without any discernible distinction), teddy bear and nostalgia is Oxford's most-read poet, although in many ways Auden is

Oxford's most distinguished poet. He too got a third.

As Solzhenitsyn has said: 'Literature transmits incontrovertible condensed experience . . . from generation to generation. In this way literature becomes the living memory of a nation.' Oxford literature continues to represent – not just for the people who were there, but for the world at large – something almost mystical. Oxford is overwhelmingly a city that exists in the imagination. It's as though tens of thousands of people have seen it through a highly personal prism, and its writers have undoubtedly contributed to the reverie. All cities have many personalities and sometimes these are shaped by writers: Dickens, for example, is as closely identified with London as any writer with a city. The test is not whether the writer wrote well about a city, but whether the city has come to define itself in terms of the writing. Oxford will for ever be tied to Waugh and hobbled by Waugh.

When I arrived at Oxford I was assailed by the sense, as Oscar Wilde put it, of the conjunction between beauty and ideas, as though the stones themselves were speaking to me. And this, too, I see in Berlin and von Trott. Berlin claimed to have no eye at all, but it is clear that from the first, as a rather chubby boy from Hollycroft Avenue in Hampstead, the son of immigrants from Riga, he responded to Oxford with passion. It doesn't take everybody this way. Where the believer sees an astonishing mix of honeyed buildings, breathing its accumulated wisdom gently, the agnostic sees smugness and reaction and damp, unfit accommodation. In my first term I remember a very tall, angular basketball player from Yale sitting huddled over a blow-heater of a design long forgotten, a sort of curved metal box with a grille at the top that produced a thin warmish breeze. He could not believe the primitiveness of a system that demanded shillings to be fed into a meter. I, of course, found this kind of thing charming.

Berlin, who loved gossip and feared himself to be a dilettante, good only for endless conversation, proved to be a more substantial figure. The moment – presaged by his strong stand against von Trott's letter – when he realised that he understood at a deep level what was going on in Europe, and what the consequences were for his study of the history of ideas, his realisation that values can be utterly incompatible and that human beings cannot be shaped to every end, seems to me to have been the tipping point. In 1933 Berlin quoted Kant in a letter to the novelist Elizabeth Bowen to the effect that: 'Out of the crooked timber of humanity no straight thing was ever made.' It became one of his favourite sayings. The logical consequence of such a belief is that there can be no perfect society. Thirties Europe was, he saw, trembling between two competing and exclusive visions of a perfect society, one Communist, one Fascist, and both deluded.

Long before I reached university in Johannesburg, aged seventeen, it was very obvious that in South Africa the prescriptive idea of society, one based furthermore on fascism and race, was still alive. When I read *Two Concepts of Liberty*, I saw that this was about all totalitarian societies, not about what happened in Russia or Germany. I could see now that I could both loathe apartheid and fear the ideologues who believed that Marx and Lenin or Mao had the answers, that they had broken the code or discovered an incorrigible proposition. In fact it was these *dirigistes*, Berlin suggested, who were the true enemies of freedom, by their insistence on 'freedom' through the state. So Oxford was for me the incarnation of liberalism, not just the home of duffel coats and port and college rugger. I had seen the brutalities of apartheid and knew that the security forces had had a dead dog delivered as a warning to my father's offices at the liberal *Rand Daily Mail*, where he was editor. (Characteristically he didn't at the time tell my mother or my brother and me, to avoid alarming us.) So the Oxford of the sixties was indeed – apologies to Geza Vermes – like waking up in heaven. Let me say here, before I become too sententious, that I did nothing very seriously at Oxford except drink and talk, play sports and read. But I passed those years happily free from the heavy burden of being a white South African, secure in the knowledge that liberalism was not a wishy-washy form of self-delusion, and that political quietism is perfectly acceptable. I cling to this belief all these years later.

Oxford is not one thing: it takes everybody differently. But I think it is undeniably true that Oxford is part of the fabric of the Anglophone world. Harold Bloom, Yale professor and Shakespeare fanatic, said to me – I was interviewing him in New York – that Shakespeare *is* our culture, that we are all his children. I think you could make a case for saying that Oxford, too, is similarly inseparable from our world and our culture.

And yet it is still a surprise to me, as it was in 1965, to find after a short journey from London that Oxford is still there, a city of enchantment, not on a plain, of course, but in a damp valley; every time I pass over Magdalen Bridge I think of Isaiah Berlin and Adam von Trott striding around Addison's Walk just across the river to the right, talking, talking, talking, something Marlowe described five hundred years ago so aptly as 'walking, disputing, et cetera'.

3

In October 1965 I was arrested in Madrid. I had just spent the summer conducting American tourists around Europe. As I had never been to Europe, it was a process of education for all of us. I travelled in the front of the bus with a Baedeker open on my knees. On my last tour, before I was due at Oxford, I arrived at Barajas Airport, Madrid, without a visa. South Africans were required to have visas in many countries, but I had failed to appreciate that Spain was one of them. I could not abandon my party and I had – typically – been speaking knowledgeably about Madrid. In fact the closest I had ever come to Madrid was a small part in Lorca's *The Blood Wedding*, at university in Johannesburg. So while they were holding me at the airport, I slipped out through the kitchens when nobody was looking and took a taxi to the hotel. At four in the morning the Guardia Civil came for me and I was put on a plane to Paris. Forty tourists were left in Madrid to fend for themselves. The thing I remember most vividly about being ordered out of bed by two heavily armed policemen is that one of them said how young I was. Perhaps he had thought they had been sent to arrest a big-time criminal.

Anyway, I decided to go to Oxford to find Trinity, my college, and bed myself in. Term had started and I was late, but, because of my fortuitous arrest, only by a day or two. I think now that I lived in something of a fog, thanks to an inability to take small details – visa, term-time and so on – seriously. In fact I had been to Trinity for an interview earlier in the year, but now I was at last an Oxford man. I put myself down for the rugby trials and played, without any training, at Iffley Road and found that there were a few international players in the A team. One of them ran right over me without apparently realising I was there, rather like a motorist running over a vole. In the Iffley Road changing rooms a coal fire burned. The ghost of Roger Bannister hung over the place, although of course he was, and is, very much alive. In our family the

Four-minute Mile was a legend, up there with the Conquest of Everest.

I had been accepted to read PPE, which sounded rather sophisticated to me in Johannesburg. I quickly discovered that I had done most of the philosophy and politics on offer, but I also found I was having great difficulty in understanding economics. I had a tutor in another college who made it brutally clear that he thought I would probably never understand economics. I told him that, as far as I could make out, economics was just a matter of having a policy and hoping for the best. Our relationship had no future: I understood quickly that one of the disadvantages of the tutorial system was that if you didn't get on with your tutor you had nowhere to hide.

John Betjeman loathed his tutor, C.S. Lewis, and Lewis, as his diaries reveal, loathed Betjeman: 'I wish I could get rid of the idle prig. I was rung up on the telephone . . . from Moreton in the Marsh, to say that he hasn't been able to read the OE, as he was suspected for measles & forbidden to look at a book. Probably a lie, but what can one do?' Once Betjeman 'appeared in a pair of eccentric bedroom slippers and said he hoped I didn't mind them, as he had a blister.

He seemed so pleased with himself that I couldn't help replying that I should mind them very much myself but I had no objection to *his* wearing them.' C.S. Lewis was particularly annoyed by Betjeman's contention that Lord Alfred Douglas, Wilde's lover, was a great writer. Betjeman for the rest of his life blamed Lewis for his failure to get a degree, which needed a pass in divinity – 'failed in divvers' was his lament in one of his poems. Although Lewis did not inspire Betjeman, he did attract another generation, people like poet and novelist John Wain.

I decided that I should get out of PPE fast. I was, surprisingly, given permission to change to a graduate degree, a BLitt in politics. But first I had to find a supervisor, the graduate version of a tutor, only seen infrequently. Nobody seemed to mind that I was floating free in Oxford without one. I can't remember how I came to choose Oliver Cromwell as a subject, but it might have been the result of a guerrilla raid on Trinity Library, because I still have a volume of Cromwell's letters which it is now probably too late to return.

Eventually, by a typically Oxford process of informal hints and suggestion, I found John

Plamenatz at Nuffield. He was a fellow of All Souls and a Montenegrin; as it happens I had read one of his books, which was a set work in South Africa. He knew nothing about Cromwell, but a lot about Tito, who had absorbed the Kingdom of Montenegro into Yugoslavia. This modest handicap to a fruitful relationship was never discussed. When I am, occasionally, invited to speak to student groups, I see that students more and more require something very specific from university: skills and certificates that they can put to good use in their careers. Yet at Oxford the idea that learning is an end in itself still persists in surprising ways. But the idea that the Classics equipped the best brains for anything life could throw at them – still persistent, if treated a little ironically in the sixties – is more or less dead and buried. With a four-year degree in Classics, known as Greats, you could confidently advance into the jungle to administer the lives of thousands. Now Classics has a new status, as a back-door entry to Oxford, because few state schools teach Latin or Greek.

That first term I felt that Oxford corresponded to something I had known in another life. There was a morphine-addicted South African writer, Eugene Marais, who claimed that we have a phyletic memory, a memory we don't even know we have. (Another South African writer, Laurens Van der Post, believed something similar.) This, I thought, is it: I have recovered my memory. That first October, the shadows lengthening and then fading on the Front Quad, the bells pealing all over Oxford, figures cycling by in what I took to be a distracted, intellectual fashion through the thickening gloom, the soft halation of lights on walls, I had the overwhelming feeling that life had just begun. Oxford instantly gave me a sense that I was at last where I was supposed to be. I was aware, of course, that I wasn't the first person to suffer Oxford's version of Jerusalem syndrome.

In *Zuleika Dobson*, Max Beerbohm writes that the Germans didn't like Oxford at all, the Americans didn't like it enough and the colonials liked it too much. I fell unmistakably into the last category. My father had given me a hirsute tweed suit that would have stopped bullets, and I teamed this with a pink polo-necked shirt from Blades, which had a zip down the back. I began, for reasons I can't now justify, or understand, to pretend that my family owned a gold mine. In fact by this stage my father was a comparatively impecunious journalist. He was a man whose wartime service in the Royal Navy worked a magical effect on him; for the rest of his life he wore a pinstriped suit in the African heat and spoke with no discernible South African accent. Now I think we are similar, always eager to impress, always trying to discover where the centre of things is located. Yet at Oxford that first term in my tweed suit, playing rugby for the college team, eating crumpets afterwards and then drinking too much in the White Horse next door, I still, I think, retained a sense of irony, a sense that I was consciously taking part in a parody, something my father would never have done. It may be that for all his English-gentleman persona, he had failed to encounter irony, which was certainly the prevailing posture of the sixties. Despite this play-acting, I think it is the happiest I have ever been, an ecstasy that I will never experience again.

In his freshers' speech, Michael Beloff referred to the tutorial system, sometimes described as 'the jewel in the crown' of Oxford and Cambridge. The idea that as an undergraduate you can spend an hour or two a week with one of the finest minds in Oxford – maybe even in England – expert in your subject, is seductive. So it has come as a surprise to discover that the tutorial system is the product of the Victorian reforms of Oxford: I had assumed it was something time-honoured and venerable. But the history of the tutorial is, like so much else in England, a series of unplanned advances and retreats. So lazy, drink-sodden and self-serving had many fellows of colleges become by the middle of the nineteenth century – a majority of them didn't even live in Oxford – that private tutors had to be found outside the colleges for the intellectually curious. When the university reforms were introduced in 1852 and 1854 these private tutors, who had set up shop all over Oxford, were eventually brought into the colleges not out of the sudden realisation that one-to-one teaching was desirable, but to bring the standards up. Oxford was deep in a trough. Matthew Arnold wrote: 'Beautiful city! So venerable, so lovely, so unravaged by the fierce intellectual life of our century, so serene.' Incidentally, it was he who described the place as 'home of lost causes', a phrase that continues, 'and forsaken beliefs, and unpopular names, and impossible loyalties'.

By the end of the nineteenth century Oxford, with Balliol leading the way, had become the intellectual (and semi-spiritual) powerhouse of the nation and empire. What we think of now as being typically Oxonian was in fact fashioned in a relatively brief period of time. Throughout the second half of the century Oxford was in a ferment of religious schism, of nationalistic fervour and scientific excitement. Newman, from my own college, and his colleagues began to issue tracts about the need for spiritual renewal, and this was to be known as the Oxford Movement. He became Vicar of St Mary's, the university church, where his preaching attracted wide interest. He and his friends, John Keble, Richard Froude and Edward Pusey, the other great names of this revival, and their tracts had, for a while, enormous influence. They were, in many ways, odd: Pusey's wife beat their children unmercifully, tying them to the bedpost for whole days for their spiritual good. Pusey's first tract was on the spiritual benefits of fasting. Newman fell in love with Froude, while at the same time turning against science: he believed that the purpose of Oxford was to guide and purify the Church. The Church was a branch of state, the ministry of morals, and he felt Oxford had a special duty in this respect.

Like Gerard Manley Hopkins, when Newman became a Roman Catholic he took orders and left Oxford for ever when he could no longer maintain his all-male establishment – a monastery in all but name – at Littlemore, which he had founded in 1842. Hair shirts and whips were kept at Littlemore for use by the acolytes. Newman's *Apologia Pro Vita Sua* was intended to have an echo of *Confessions* by Augustine, and has been highly regarded for a century or more. A recent biography of Newman suggests that the asceticism of many of the early members of the Oxford Movement was a refuge for a homosexual clique, which clung to male monasticism and excessive devotion as a kind of reaction to their own torments. Homosexuality was, of course, anathema to the religious. By the fourth quarter of the century there were a number of cautiously homosexual Oxford writers, notably John Addington Symonds, once of Balliol, who had become known for writing – sometimes secretly, sometimes in the guise of classical studies – about homosexuality, although he too was personally troubled by it: he believed it was curable. In later years he spent his life between Davos, where he was a patron of the local sports club, and Venice. He said of his Venetian lover, 'I gave him a gondola.' But it seems certain that there was a powerful undercurrent in Oxford of what was thought of as perversion and it seems likely that the Oxford Movement provided an alternative for those who wished to deal with the question of their perceived sexual sinfulness. As Michael Beloff hinted in his address to the freshers, it might be some time before Newman's beatification takes place.

It was a time of immense, even epic, change and debate in Oxford. The rise of science was particularly challenging to the old order, which believed, rather like fundamentalists today, that everything we needed to know about the natural world was contained in the scriptures. At least in part as a consequence of the predominance of its religious and classical reactionaries, Oxford had a lot of ground to make up in the sciences: in 1850 there are said to have been less than forty living graduates in medicine from Oxford in the entire Empire. The Dean of Christ Church at the time of Darwin explained to his students: 'Nor can I do better than impress upon you the study of Greek literature, which not only elevates above the vulgar herd, but leads not infrequently to positions of considerable emolument.'

The point of this is that Oxford, in contrast to Cambridge, is still temperamentally inclined towards the arts, Classics and politics while Cambridge is more at home with the sciences, medicine and architecture. (Although Mrs Thatcher's cabinet had a number of Cambridge graduates.) In 1970, nearly seventy-five per cent of all Oxford undergraduates were studying an arts subject, although in the last thirty-five years there has been a levelling off. There are other measures that suggest that Oxford is still behind, such as the disproportionately large numbers of Nobel Prizes in the sciences won by Cambridge, the size of the Cambridge medical faculty (220 undergraduates against 150 at Oxford) and the prestige of its science establishment, notably the Cavendish Laboratory founded in 1874. But Oxford, after a slow start, recognised the importance of science and with the appointment in 1919 of Frederick Lindemann as head of the Clarendon Laboratory, developed a formidable reputation in the sciences. Lindemann was a German who had made possible some of Einstein's deductions with his early work in physics.

In more recent times, Oxford has had many notable successes in chemistry, physics and medicine, including Howard Florey's and Ernst Chain's discovery of penicillin, which has had a far more beneficent effect on the world than Archie and Aloysius (note the coded reference to Anglo-Catholic Oxford). Florey was an Australian and Chain was a refugee from Nazi Germany. They shared with Alexander Fleming the Nobel in 1945. Between the war and 1975, Oxford scientists were awarded six Nobel Prizes compared with only six to the whole of France. In fact there has been a substantial shift to the sciences, with St Catherine's leading the way. But still Oxford retains its reputation as an arts-dominated university. Part of the problem is that some science dons have often been *non-dons*, that is to say teachers without a college fellowship, which tends to suggest that they belong to the second team, and that has been a source of discontent. There were soon mutterings about the requirement for scientists to pass a Latin exam, something that Oxford clung to into the sixties as a condition of matriculation.

At the same time it is easily demonstrated that Oxford has produced far more prime ministers, newspaper editors and literary critics than Cambridge. (Although under Leavis's influence as editor of *Scrutiny*, Cambridge forged ahead in the field of literary criticism in the thirties, forties and fifties.) Half of all the nineteen prime ministers since 1900 have come from Oxford. Tony Blair, although manifestly in touch with the sentimental aspect of contemporary society and adept at the language of feeling, is identifiably an Oxford man, with a kind of self-deprecating superiority. His familiarity with the media and his understanding of news management are hardly surprising: to this day Oxford has a virtual monopoly of the top newspaper and publishing jobs in London, which are intimately entwined. There is a well-worn path that leads from reading English and practising student journalism at Oxford to a gophering job on a newspaper, assisting the literary editor, before moving on to publishing the first novel, or into publishing itself. This path is made easier because between Oxford writers there is 'cordial mutuality in books and texts in the way that these authors dedicate poems to each other, drop each other's names, feature each other as characters, share allusions, swap private jokes', as Valentine Cunningham puts it in his contribution to *The History of the University of Oxford*. Many Oxford-originated magazines have come and gone over the years, but *Private Eye* is the child of *Parson's Pleasure*, founded by Richard Ingrams and Paul Foot in Oxford in 1959.

Although I was always aware that I could write with some facility, I was not aware while I was at Oxford of the tracks through the literary undergrowth, probably because I had, perversely, chosen the social sciences. My mind, anyway, was on film and television: I wanted to direct films. Every time I went into a cinema I came out burning with a longing to make films. I had ideas about African films that would locate someone – a version of myself – with a highly developed sensibility in an African setting. In fact some years later I wrote a short television play that involved just such a person, and the BBC filmed it. Later in advertising I made commercials, but before moving on to documentaries, I made one feature film. My feature-film career began and ended with *Rosie Dixon, Night Nurse*, which I drew on for my novel, *White Lightning*. Stephen Frears, I think it was, said that when you become a film director you become an expert on haircuts. With *Rosie Dixon* it was underwear. I remember a meeting with the wardrobe lady to look at and discuss upwiring for our woefully under-equipped leading lady. Nothing I had learned at Oxford helped with this problem.

It was only while preparing for this book, by reading the Franks Report of 1966 and other investigations, and by interviewing Oxford dons, that I became aware that the tutorial system is seen as a mixed blessing. While surveys show that undergraduates want to keep it, the teaching fellows are not united. But they understand that the system is a very real part of Oxford's appeal, even though it is estimated that every undergraduate costs every college five thousand pounds a year. In those sciences where tutorials still exist, some tutors have to repeat the same basic knowledge five or six times a week, where one seminar would do. I was surprised when Valentine Cunningham told me that the classic tutorial has not existed since the mid-sixties: he anyway prefers a seminar, believing that he can get far more done and that the brightest students lead the way.

But there is something enormously seductive about the idea of one-to-one teaching even if sometimes the one-to-one is actually one-to-two or -three. Still, the basic requirement for an undergraduate is an average of one and a half essays a week. The system has, I discovered, another advantage: no undergraduate can slip through the net without being noticed. Emailed excuses and alibis quickly find out the lazy and the evasive or reveal the troubled.

At Trinity I met a young English don, Simon Humphries, who seemed on first acquaintance to represent the new wave. He was, for example, wearing a T-shirt in the Fellows' Dining Room. The Fellows' Dining Room is a lovely panelled room – only God knows how many lovely panelled rooms there are in Oxford – where fellows of the college eat lunch and dinner if they want to. There are fewer single dons left living in college than there used to be, so lunch tends to be the main communal meal. The food in Trinity has always been good. In Wolfson, a deliberately democratic place, the food on daily offer is very poor. The connection between the traditional Oxford colleges and dining is a strange and elastic one, but there is probably no other university in the world, apart from Cambridge, that sees meals in the same way, as a fusion of the traditional monastic community and the aristocratic habits of a century ago. I think there is something provocative about it: *This is the way we do it, and we are not going to change*. Of course it plays very well out in the world of publishing and politics and law and hedge funds where the undergraduates are headed.

I asked Simon Humphries if he would be prepared to take me for a tutorial, setting me an essay and criticising it without fear or favour. He said he would and eventually we were able to fix a time. I decided that I would try, as far as possible, to rely on my own literary knowledge and what I had learnt in twenty years of reading and reviewing to write the essay. I saw a problem looming: my reviewing has largely been of contemporary novels. Simon was disconcertingly vague about what I was to do: he would be giving me some extracts to read; I was to make of them what I could. The last thing he wanted was for me to Google literary theory or look at Oxford examination questions. What method, I asked tentatively, do you advocate in Oxford these days? Close reading, he said. This appeared to be the Oxford version of deconstruction, with all the highly theoretical French elements removed. Essentially, I guessed, close reading meant not taking anything at face value. But under my self-imposed restrictions, I wasn't able to take advice. I should have.

The Faculty of English Admissions Criteria include enthusiasm for literature, sensitivity to the creative use of language, intellectual curiosity, conceptual clarity, critical engagement, flexibility, accuracy, attention to details, capacity for hard work and articulacy. Certainly on items one to three I felt I was qualified, with perhaps some doubt about critical engagement and capacity for hard work. Simon had said that he was going to be more nervous than I was, but I was pretty sure that, once I was within his pedagogic force-field, I would quickly be put in place. I remembered John Updike writing that at reunions you quickly assumed the role and position you had had back at school. And I had always been, until exams anyway, slightly under-prepared and superficial.

One of the problems of the tutorial system is that because of the burden of writing as many as three essays a week, and the open-ended nature of essays, many undergraduates present rushed work. Only a few have the time to marshal a fraction of the supporting evidence for the argument and even fewer can produce originality. Yet that is precisely what the tutorial system is supposed to encourage. So I decided to further limit myself to about two days' work.

The extracts Simon had given me to consider were interesting: a piece from John Ruskin's *Of Kings Treasuries from Sesame and Lilies*, 'Stepping Westward', by William Wordsworth, 'It Was a Hard Thing', by Gerard Manley Hopkins, 'The Knight in the Wood', by Lord de Tabley, and 'Old China', an essay by Charles Lamb. As far as I could remember, I had never read any of these except for the Lamb, although the first time I was aware of the power of poetry, as opposed to the comforts of childish rhyme and doggerel, was when I read 'Tintern Abbey'. The hedges that had become sportive woods were, to a South African boy, an intriguing mystery. It seemed barely possible that a whole country could be divided by picturesque hedgerows. In fact many things in our culture did not correspond to what we actually saw around us: we celebrated Guy Fawkes' and Christmas and snow and fir trees, but hedgerows were a step too far for the imagination.

I had recently read a biography of Lamb's friend Hazlitt, I knew a little about Hopkins and Ruskin, but as far as I could remember I had never read a word by Lord de Tabley, or ever heard of him. I read Simon's pieces through and

I began to wonder if they were exercises in seeing beyond the obvious. Simon, I thought, was asking me to look behind the arras and see what the pieces were really about. Close reading, in fact.

When I came back to Oxford a week or two later, I had prepared a few pages to read to Simon. He was waiting in his new study, looking out over a small garden towards Front Quad, a perfectly framed view, a distillation of Oxford. It seemed to me, after my labours, that the academic life in a subject as wide as English literature is astonishingly liberating. You are free, in fact you are required, to explore ideas that have little or no obvious application but that contain in one way or another the whole imagined world. I review a fair number of books every year, but the job as I see it is to give the occasional reader a summary of the book, some context, and then simply to advise him or her if I think the book is worth buying. But for the teaching academic the job is very different; it is to read and interpret, and to take account of academic thinking, research, social history and the shifting drifts of literary theory, in order to draw from the student some deep response to literature. There is no question that unread books make us anxious; nothing is more depressing for the professional writer to find one's intelligent friends reading rubbish when there are so many great books waiting unread. However diligent you may be, there is always a feeling that there is a steepling bookcase of unread books looming, ready to fall on your head. In reality I would guess that English dons at Oxford don't read day and night: journals, the *Times Literary Supplement* and the *New York Review of Books* probably keep them on the alert. Harold Bloom, in the interview I mentioned earlier, told me some wonderfully libellous stories of colleagues in American universities who had never read Milton or Shakespeare. One thing the Franks Commission discovered, rather to their surprise, was that Oxford dons have the highest rate of publication in the whole world of academe.

With Simon, I was aware from the first moment of a very extensive reading behind him. He had started life as a librarian and came to Oxford as a mature student, without any academic qualifications, and went on to take a first in English.

I began to read my essay. I started with Ruskin's:

> Very ready we are to say of a book, 'How good this is – that's exactly what I think!' But the right feeling is, 'How strange that is! I never thought of that before, and yet I see it is true; or if I do not now, I hope I shall, some day.' But whether thus submissively or not, at least be sure that you go to the author to get at his meaning, not to find yours.

I have been using a sentiment much like this as a definition of literature, as opposed to genre fiction, that literature produces the sense that we have intuited something similar but never heard it expressed in this way. Literature, in this fashion, increases the human understanding. I explained this, and moved on. But I saw immediately that I had passed too lightly over Ruskin's prescription of how to attack an author's work: I had ignored, for example, as Simon soon told me, Ruskin's reference to a writer's reluctance to give the meaning of his work too readily: Ruskin refers to writing in parables. Simon asked me if I had wondered why he used the word 'parables'. I had a feeling of drowning; I had simply passed by on the other side, taking it to be a reference to imagery. Simon suggested it might be a direct scriptural reference to Mark IV, in which Jesus says he speaks in parables so that men may not understand. Already I was feeling apprehensive of what was to come. I had given two paragraphs to Ruskin and made a fairly easy point that Graham Greene in his essays had said something similar about the correct way to respond to a piece of literature, which is not, 'How good this is – that's exactly what I think', as Ruskin put it, but, 'How strange this is!' I now find that Auden said much the same thing, and of course Greene would have read Auden.

Worse, I had fatally ignored the parable and with it the most significant thing about the piece, which is that writers deliberately withhold meaning. In my own experience of novelists it is true that they have, as Ruskin says, 'cruel reticence . . . which makes them hide their deeper light'. In an interview with Craig Raine, David Lodge makes the same point, that novelists are reluctant to get right down to the bedrock of their ideas, for fear of revealing the poverty or banality of their sources. I have found that audiences often ask where I get my ideas, as if that is the only thing they are missing in their own writing. As I was reading, it struck me that just the two pages of Ruskin could have produced a much more detailed and interesting essay than the wafer-thin criticism I was now offering on all five pieces. My confidence was low as I saw how I had misjudged the whole thing. I clung, however, to the idea that the limits I had set myself were the reason for my failure.

We moved on to 'Stepping Westward', by Wordsworth. I knew by now that my two paragraphs – longish – would be hopelessly inadequate. For those of you, like me, who have no memory of reading this poem, it starts in striking fashion: 'What, are you stepping Westward? – Yea.' Wordsworth is on a walk through Scotland with Dorothy. But I had missed entirely references to Milton and the change of person: the initial '*we* who thus together roam' had become by the end of the poem *me* who is travelling through the world on his endless way. Keats, Simon told me, had believed Wordsworth egotistical, and Wordsworth did not believe Dorothy had his ability to fix what was permanent and universal in verse; the *we* was dropped for the intellectual section of the poem.

And so the tutorial proceeded to Hopkins's 'It Was a Hard Thing'. I was able to summon from memory Hopkins's 'inscape' – the imperative to discover the essential quality of things. While I was writing the essay I felt I had discovered the essential qualities of Simon's brief, but now I was not so sure. In fact, Simon suggested that Hopkins's aesthetic was anti-romantic. Perhaps this was supposed to be an essay about the Romantics, I thought wildly, but in truth I now had no idea at all.

Lord de Tabley, a Victorian poet Simon had studied closely, was, I thought, banal, and his poem, 'The Knight in the Wood', proclaiming a rough carving in an Italian museum far superior to the 'rose sentimentalities' of Guido and Dolce (I have to say Dolce and Gabbana came to mind), I dismissed as promoting intensity of feeling over art. It is, I thought, an example of lazy romanticism. But again – I knew it was coming – I had missed some vital pointers. For all that, I stick to my first impression that this is a load of tosh.

I did better with 'Old China', by Charles Lamb. Simon said that he would have to reconsider his view of the essay in the light of my suggestion that Lamb draws the reader into a satirical trap, which is sprung much later in the piece. I was pleased to be complimented, after decades of writing, with nine novels and hundreds of reviews and essays published, by young Simon. But I had a rather depressing image of Simon re-reading his Charles Lamb. The gloom that this image cast was not on Simon, but on me. I can think of no time in my life when I will read any of the books I own again – apart from Saul Bellow – unless it is for journalistic or reference purposes.

I left Trinity, shaken by Simon's judgement that, if I were a first year, he would say, 'Must read more attentively.' I walked down to Magdalen, and did a tour of Addison's Walk, and I dwelt on the idea that the tutorial system, and Oxford, can still offer the incomparable pleasures of pure thought. As a writer, despite some of the insecurities and disappointments of the life, I am able to spend hours every week in libraries, although often my thoughts and researches are directed by the novel I am writing or the review I am working on. But I found my tutorial surprisingly inspiring. Even now I would like to read Victorian poetry and criticism at the whim of a tutor and then have a lively conversation about it. I have since read about Hopkins and the Catholic revival in English literature, and Jonathan Wordsworth on 'Tintern Abbey' and other poems. *The Lakeland Journals* are waiting.

I also asked Geza Vermes about Mark IV, because I wanted to see, not if Simon was wrong about parables, but whether Ruskin was. Geza referred me to his book, *The Authentic Gospel of Jesus*. He also sent me an email:

> Mark and Matthew take the word 'parable' to mean 'riddle'. In fact it can mean anything from a wisdom saying, to a simile, a parable or a puzzle. Jews used parables as a teaching medium, a colourful illustration of something abstract. Non-Jewish audiences found them tough and needed a lot of explanation. In the Gospels the apostles, like the later Gentiles, are portrayed as pretty dense.

In his book Geza writes: 'The truth is that preaching of the parables had different effects on listeners or readers whether they were Jews or Gentiles.' The Evangelists had inserted the idea that Jesus deliberately obscured the truth, which could only be perceived by true believers.

Now this makes absolutely no difference to my interpretation of Ruskin's meaning, but what it seems to suggest to me is that a lifetime of scholarship could easily go by in exploring these highways and byways. I had learned a few years before, for example, that the commentaries on the Dead Sea Scrolls by the Essenes of Qumran were not written as history, but as interpretation of prophecies: the Hellenic tradition, which we think of as the beginnings of historicism, was unknown to the religious. It seems to me that in fundamentalist circles it still is. And Ruskin believed that all art must have a spiritual dimension. Yet there is obviously an argument for saying – if Geza Vermes is correct – that Ruskin's view of the writer's motives was formed by a mistaken understanding of the Gospels. The idea that Jesus deliberately spoke in a way designed to confuse was a much later interpretation by the Evangelists writing in Greek and unfamiliar with the rabbinic and Aramaic traditions of someone like Jesus, a Galilean healer and preacher.

W.H. Auden's relationship with Oxford came in three intalments in three very different decades, the first as a glittering undergraduate in 1925, the second as Professor of Poetry in 1956, admired, inspiring and a figure of great importance, holding court in the Cadena tea rooms in Cornmarket. Tom Paulin recently described Auden (and MacNeice), using a phrase of Eliot's, as possessing lyrical grace and tough eloquence. When he returned to Oxford in 1972 to live in a cottage provided by Christ Church, another Auden appeared – old, rambling, rather embittered, as he tried to re-establish his little salon in St Aldate's Coffee House. In some ways his life seems to be a paradigm of the Oxford experience, from golden youth to disillusionment in a few decades, and a life lived in the refracted light of the enclosed world of Oxford, expressed in his poem 'Oxford'. As Valentine Cunningham puts it:

> However much the poem might protest that this 'outside' matters, it too fails to break the seductive grip of the enclosure, the magnetic hold on the imagination of a magical place, this formative Oxford matrix that remains afterwards for so many of its alumni (and alumnae), both writing and non-writing ones, a decisive and inerasable part of the self.

Auden's most famous lines about Oxford are these:

Nature is so near; the rooks in the college
  gardens
Like agile babies, still speak the language of
  feeling.
By the tower the river still runs to the sea,
  and will run,
    And the stones in that tower are utterly
    Satisfied with their weight.

Because I was curious to see how he would respond, I asked Simon Humphries how he interpreted Auden's poem. I wanted to know what Auden was saying about Oxford. Simon's reply was comprehensive and fascinating and gave me some clues as to where I had gone wrong in my tutorial. He started by asking me which version of the poem I was reading – Auden revised some of his poems – and went on to explain that, at the time he wrote the poem, Auden was preoccupied with Freud and concerned about the nature/culture dualism. It's not so much about Oxford as about Vienna. The line in the poem about rooks talking the language of feeling produced from Simon a virtuoso explanation of the carelessness of nature – that is to say, its lack of interest in humans, and the concept of akedia or accidia, something he connects to Virgil's 'Purgatoria', which he assumes Auden is familiar with. He then quoted an Auden essay on Housman that seemed to support his thesis that Auden was deeply interested in the varieties of dualism that plague the thinking man. Outside the colleges, Auden suggests, 'ordinary' people simply get on with their lives. As Simon concludes, 'A more ambitious piece than its title might make us expect.'

I suspected that that last remark was aimed straight at my heart; a reproach to the careless, rather superficial fashion in which I have treated literature and culture, always aware of the trends and the cant, but not always as widely read as I have pretended, often under the pressure of making a living. Close reading, I see now, is the antidote to all this.

Auden, I think, was an unattractive character, at heart deeply cynical, although many who knew him record his loyalty to friends. In reading about Auden, I saw that his Will indicated that he knew all along what Anthony Blunt, Keeper of the Queen's Pictures and spy, was about: 'Item, I leave my friend Anthony Blunt a copy of Marx and £1,000 a year. And the picture of *Love Locked Out* by Holman Hunt.' Auden, like Philby, Burgess, Maclean and Blunt, had, I think, a sort of disgust for the privilege that they were never quite able to forget or forsake.

I was strongly attracted by the idea that I could have lived another existence altogether here in Oxford, walking and disputing. All too late, all hopeless, of course, but it struck me that one of the aspects of Oxford that never leaves us is the sense that we were, for a few years, in touch with a world where ideas have value for their own sake. When a recent Home Secretary described medievalists as having ornamental value, I was saddened. Is it possible to understand our culture by ignoring whole chunks of history or by denigrating the work of specialists in certain arcane subjects? That way lies the sterile, closed society, exactly the sort of place that breeds materialism, intellectual superficiality and religious fundamentalism. The tutorial system, by design or accident, is addressed directly to the questioning of received wisdom and the probing of meaning.

But there are limits to the tutorial system. As I had found, one of these is that being tied to a tutor for a term or a year may be onerous for both parties. Some tutors are bored by tutorials: as Hugh Trevor-Roper put it: 'I firmly and conveniently believe that undergraduates really only learn by teaching themselves.' At Oxford there is really no mechanism for getting rid of inadequate tutors, although it is possible for the undergraduate to ask to be assigned to another tutor in another college. The system is under threat because of the need for students to leave with a piece of paper that reads 2:1 or 1; anything less is thought by many to be a disgrace. The result of this is that there is pressure to prepare students for exams rather than for a life of elevated thought.

Benjamin Jowett, probably Oxford's most famous head of a college, had aimed to use the tutorial to 'inoculate England with Balliol'. When a Professor Blackie of Glasgow University wrote to him: 'I hope you in Oxford don't think we hate you,' Jowett replied: 'We don't think of you at all.' Oxford was 'the granary of intellectual and spiritual life', wrote J.A. Smith. 'Nothing,' he said, 'will be of any use to you except this, you should be able to detect when a man is talking rot.' And Beerbohm described the typical Oxford man of the time as possessing a 'playful and caressing suavity of manner', developed at least partly by the tutorial. In Jowett's mind, worldly success was everything: 'I have a great prejudice,' he said, 'against all those who do not succeed in the world.' His other dictum: 'Never retreat. Never explain. Get it done and let them howl' was based on the belief that the tutorial system had developed particular worldly aptitudes. But for Jowett this material success was to be achieved in the imperial project, in the Law and the Commons, not in an investment bank or by becoming a partner in some solicitors' firm dealing with the City and its superfluity of money; there was something of the moral enquiry about Oxford tutorials, the better to discover idealism and patriotism. The last generation that never escaped the quad is just passing. It is marked by a love of formal dining and dressing up and by knowing and complicit speeches, which give a sense that the true élite of the country do indeed possess a caressing wit.

I think one can see pretty clearly where Oxford finds itself now: the tutorial is much prized, particularly by undergraduates, but it is prized more as cultural capital, part and parcel of the whole Oxford experience, than for its own sake, although I don't think anybody could deny that a fondness for the essay, followed by the vigorous discussion, is visible at the top levels of the

Civil Service, in the Cabinet and in the adversarial nature of Parliament and High Court: they are the children of the tutorial system and conditioned by the quad. Every report by some distinguished judge or retired civil servant reads like an extended essay, concerned with advertising a higher intellect as much as with the matter in hand. As Naylor says in Cyril Connolly's *The Rock Pool* of a friend from Oxford days: 'Spedding had simply exchanged the Gothic quads, dining-halls, gowns, subfusc pleasures and gregarious intolerance of Winchester and Oxford for those of the law courts. He would never leave the quadrangle.'

Isaiah Berlin claimed in conversation with his biographer, Michael Ignatieff, that his philosophy tutor at Corpus Christi, Frank Hardie, had stripped away all his superficial notions and taught him how to get to the essentials: 'Obscurity and pretentiousness and sentences which doubled over themselves he wrung right out of me, from then until this moment.' If it is true, we are deeply in debt to Frank Hardie: almost every time I read a book by academics, I wish they had had a tutor like Frank Hardie. Oxford's influence in the world is not as great as it was, at least not glaringly obviously so, but there are many who still see the trinity of tutorial, college and university as uniquely equipped to produce the minds and manners to keep the country somewhere near the forefront, if such a thing is actually measurable.

For all that it is less obvious, Oxford's predominance in our national life is still apparent if you know where to look. Where I live in North London, I can be reasonably sure that every fourth or fifth house in the more decorous streets will contain an Oxford barrister or an Oxford solicitor or an Oxford journalist, while a few streets away a rancorous, graffiti-disfigured, Red Bull-littered council estate will signal that we are still two nations, which tells me that those who have a tendency to blame Oxford for the fact that people from these sullen estates rarely get there – or anywhere else – are labouring under an enormous delusion. The truth is that the national average for subliteracy at the age of eleven is one in eight, and on central London estates I think you can assume that it is far higher than that. Very few children recover from that sort of start in life, but old habits of mind die hard. I have never met anyone in Britain who believes that the educational system is satisfactory. And as a colonial import, I have never had that nagging feeling, so common among the right-thinking, that Oxford's and Cambridge's relative magnificence and excellence are achieved in some way at the expense of the less privileged, and neither have I believed that the tutorial system with its expensive individual teaching is in any way to blame. There can be no connection in logic. And yet we continue to deceive ourselves.

There are, nonetheless, two factors that contribute to a widespread idea that Oxford and Cambridge are both especially favoured and especially exclusive. One is that a degree of articulacy at interview, a readiness to talk, is likely to impress an interviewer who is going to have to spend an hour a week at least with a candidate, and the other is that Oxford and Cambridge receive more government money per head than any other university, at least in part because the tutorial system is not cheap. The Senior Tutor at Trinity College, Trudy Watt, told me that silence does not help at interview. But she also stressed that the college has schools-liaison staff and that Trinity tried to overcome the attitude that 'Oxford is not for us'. Trinity was, at the time we spoke, making a special effort in the North-east. I had read in the report of the Franks Commission of 1966 the comment that Oxford does not consciously show bias, and it was exactly what Michael Beloff said forty years later: 'We discriminate neither for nor against anyone.'

The strange and disturbing fact about admissions is that the balance of state and private schools is barely more favourable to state schools than it was in 1966, although private schools only educate eight per cent of all children. State schools provide about half of the intake; the other fifty per cent contains a large number of overseas students and other categories, but it can only suggest one of two things, that Oxford favours private schools or that state education is not as good as it should be. And even the measurable change since 1966 is actually misleading, because the abolition of so many grammar schools in the period since the Franks Commission has meant that more or less the same people are coming to Oxford, but by different routes. Of course, without the option of free grammar schools, some poorer parents are not able to get the best available education for their children, so it could be argued – and has been – that the egalitarian measures introduced in the sixties have actually lessened the chances of working-class children – the Holy Grail of egalitarian thinking – getting to Oxford.

After endless conversations, my own impression is that Oxford dons are very keen to get more state school pupils in; they themselves are mostly the product of state schools, and they make allowances for the educationally deprived and try desperately to find intelligent and willing candidates. They also try to mitigate the increasing sophistication of the ambitious middle classes. Other ways of selection, involving, for example, two- and three-day tests in college, are increasingly being used, because the private schools are remarkably adept at anticipating what each college requires, to the point that candidates are even coached in the publications the dons have contributed to or originated, and candidates are occasionally briefed on the preferences and reputations of individual tutors. One tutor told me that he tries to avoid any form of work some private schools send in, just because these schools are so skilled at coaching for Oxford. He is aiming to test all candidates with a paper under exam conditions when they come in for interview, and this is likely to be a widespread practice. But even the more radical dons I have spoken to suggest that the problem lies not so much with Oxford as with the education system. In fact, every time I have had a conversation about this subject, I have been treated to a threnody about the poor standards of so much of the state sector. And this is why so many dons loathe the politicians who see an easy target that allows them to deflect the blame for a dreadful series of social and political miscalculations over the past forty years.

Nonetheless, a few pundits argue that Oxford people, however hard they try not to be, are seduced by the place and are unable to adjust to the demands or the culture of the changing society outside the quad. One critic wrote, 'They adapt, they modernise, but they do not change . . . the inestimable self-belief engendered by eight hundred years of triumph.' But the response of the dons is that Oxford must maintain high academic standards if it is to survive. Oxford has no soft options, no media studies or creative writing, for example, but it should not be forgotten that courses like PPE, when they were first introduced, attracted the same sort of opprobrium that these courses do now.

* * *

When Michael Beloff addressed the Trinity freshers he said:

> The college is one of the defining features of Oxford University. So too is the tutorial system which flourishes within a college. You have chosen this distinctive form of education. You will find that the Oxford tradition offers intimacy and friendliness – intellectual and social – which are absent from larger, more anonymous institutions.

Was he, I wondered, suggesting that the university was one of these larger and more anonymous institutions? Or was he talking about other universities where students don't have the intimacy of the college system?

Michael Beloff was a young law don at Trinity when I came up in 1965. Thirty-five years later, a hugely successful barrister, he became President of the college, and he still believes in the collegiate system and the tutorial. In fact the future of Oxford turns on these two things. The colleges, in all their enclosed glory, are said to be inward-looking and jealous of their position, and they promote themselves as the students' home and the focus of their first loyalty: 'You have come to Oxford, but it is Trinity that has admitted you,' as Beloff said. But the colleges aren't always ready to share their wealth – if they have it – and there are dark tales of colleges hiding their assets, or selling art and literary treasures for purposes that have nothing whatever to do with the welfare of the university as a whole. But then the dons would say that Oxford is one of the very few world-class institutions in Britain and it is run entirely by academics, without outside interference. And this is why the colleges don't want to hand over the lists of their alumni to the university. One college insists on having a fellow present if one of its alumni wants to donate money to the university. At least one other college has been known to shelter its money offshore so as to keep it out of the domestic accounts and so avoid paying too much into the Common University Fund, begun in 1877 expressly to help the poorer colleges. The extra cost of Oxford – the ancient buildings, the duplication of facilities – is in fact covered by the endowments, but while some colleges like St John's and Christ Church are fabulously wealthy and able to pass the benefits on to their students, others, like St Peter's, are destitute by comparison. It raises a doubt about whether all Oxford students are equal.

The question of colleges is the key one for Oxford. Can the colleges afford to have a teaching fellow in most disciplines? Can they afford to employ dons without consulting the university? Can they really be responsible for the admissions policy ahead of the university? Can they ultimately justify their autonomy from the university? In fact recently a Common Framework was introduced by the Admissions Tutors in each college, which in theory means that all colleges will apply the same criteria to admissions. But still, the latest Vice Chancellor, Dr John Hood, after a hasty and ill-judged start to his tenure, decided that in order to keep up with Harvard, Yale and Princeton, Oxford must rationalise. He said that there must be a more streamlined body than Congregation, the parliament of Oxford made up of every single fellow of the university; he proposed a management committee that would have in the end a majority of outsiders for the first time in nine hundred years. 'Outsiders' means people with business experience, and it is just this that Oxford has rejected, believing that it would introduce inside a Trojan horse the failed practices of the National Health Service and the dregs of Thatcherite philosophies. The antis were much helped by a poll that placed Oxford second behind Harvard in the world league of universities. None of the antis is suggesting that the administration of Oxford could not be improved: what they reject is the application of naked business principles to areas where they believe these outsiders have no expertise.

This time it was not about personalities, but about the dangers of embracing the idea that management and management techniques would make Oxford a better place: the National Health Service, the BBC and Enron as well as the University of Toronto's disastrous experience with a sponsor who interfered in the appointment of an academic were all cited by the opposition. Instinctively the dons believed that, once outsiders were in the majority, they would talk only to the Vice Chancellor and that top-down management would be the inevitable result. 'Education in general,' as evidence to Franks had it back in the sixties, 'and university education par excellence, are worlds in which the university administrator should be kept in his place.' I went to a meeting in London designed to support the Vice Chancellor where certain alumni were primed with questions, for example, why does the university only have the names and addresses of thirty-three per cent of the living graduates? The answer was that the colleges would not release them to the university, so thwarting the university's attempts to attract donations. But is that the real reason? Could it not be that the colleges wanted to preserve their independence and their uniqueness?

It seems clear that the Conference of Colleges, where inter-collegiate horse-trading takes place, must in the end submit to the university. In particular, says Sir Colin Lucas, the former Vice Chancellor, colleges should question the way they teach. It is simply not appropriate in many of the sciences, for example, that the colleges should have autonomy in appointments. The assumptions about culture upon which the tutorial system is based have failed to get the colleges to integrate lectures, seminars and tutorials. In other words, the colleges, for all the wonderful intimacy, must rationalise their teaching and funding.

Lucas is now Warden of Rhodes House. As we talked in the rambling Warden's Lodging designed by Herbert Baker, a sort of rectory in Rhodes's religion of empire, Lucas said to me that the Oxford reality long ago outstripped the myth. This, it is difficult not to notice, is a common complaint in Oxford now: the symbols of Oxford – the buildings, the college tradition, the tutorial system – are thought to obscure the reality of the changes and achievements of the past forty years. Colleges have changed their character in obvious ways: there are few bachelor dons living in to support the college rowing eight or rugby team, there is Broadband Internet in many rooms, and the admissions system is increasingly governed by common rules. Women and their particular talents have very clearly taken a deep hold on the colleges in the past thirty years; the colleges have been feminised, to their great benefit. (Kate Mosse, the novelist, describes the one concession New College made to the arrival of women – full-length mirrors on the staircases.)

Sciences are usually conducted in the laboratories of South Parks Road and the teaching is mostly in these labs or in seminar rooms rather than in college tutorials. Although the colleges are still largely responsible for admitting undergraduates, they have in fact had their wings clipped because the government now pays its grants directly to the university. But the college system is still very strong, and the college system makes Oxford what it is. Colleges are not just pleasant halls of residence, but centres both of teaching and research. There is no prospect of the colleges becoming specialised – say, one college for medicine, one for law and so on – something which has been suggested. But many dons and others have told me that rationalisation must take place. Some even suggest that Oxford should become a postgraduate university. A big donor to the university told me that Oxford should wake up to the realities of twenty-first-century universities: they are not museums, conservators of ancient manuscripts or preservers of custom, but the cutting edge of society. They should forget sentimentality and, as he put it, get real.

For an outsider like me, with a sentimental view of Oxford, it seems that the power of the myth of Oxford and its consequent value are underestimated by those who live and work there. The place is so beautiful, the teaching – at its best – is so wonderful, the sense of collegiality – of belonging to something ancient and serious and open-minded – is so pervasive and so richly endowed with culture that I think the natives sometimes fail to see it as the world sees it, as something unique and irreplaceable. When

I walked down Broad Street that afternoon after my tutorial, I was aware that under my feet were the great collections of the Bodleian; as I walked down Holywell, past the Music Room, I heard a pianist practising, the notes faint but distinct. From a room further down the road, from within New College, I heard someone practising the violin.

I thought of one of Isaiah Berlin's favourite novels, Turgenev's *Fathers and Sons*, and the anarchist Bazarov's repudiation of everything that was not utilitarian, beauty coming very near the top of his list. And, although I had taken something of a pasting from Simon Humphries, I thought of my tutorial and Hopkins's lines:

> The sun on falling waters writes the text
> Which yet is in the eye or in the thought.
> It was a hard thing to undo this knot.

Although I am not entirely sure, and probably will never find out, what 'this knot' is.

4

Yeats described the Bodleian Library as the friendliest and probably the most beautiful library in the world. When I applied for a reader's card as I started on this book and found that I was still on the rolls, I was immoderately moved. Why? Was it the marmalade effect, described by Harold Nicolson, who said he felt a strange frisson whenever he saw a jar labelled 'Oxford Orange Marmalade'?

No money changed hands, nobody placed any restrictions on me, nobody asked me if I had made anything of myself or beaten my wife or learned finally to get out of bed before lunchtime, and yet I was invited to inhabit this astonishing place as if, somehow, I was a part of it, as if I had never left the happy band who, since Thomas Bodley founded the place in 1598, have not just used the library, but felt themselves to be partaking of a communion. In 1610 Bodley made an agreement with the Stationers' Company to receive all new books published in Britain. The Bodleian is a library of legal deposit, a copyright library, one of only five in Britain, which means that it must receive and hold a copy of every book published in Britain, including comics and manuals. It has the first available edition, for example, of the *Eagle*. It has an astounding collection of manuscripts and papers, including the recent acquisition of Isaiah Berlin's papers; the Shakespeare Folio; most of Kafka's manuscripts; the Acts of the Apostles by the Venerable Bede; and one of the finest collections of Italian medieval manuscripts outside Italy. There are also fabulous Hebrew, Indian, Japanese and other oriental manuscripts and a fine copy of *La Chanson de Roland*. And a great deal more, including a collection of American playbills and a vast collection of ephemera, from bus tickets to advertising posters. In my delusion, I see this great, radiating – humming – collection of books and manuscripts as a sort of personal tribute to me, Bodleian Reader, rather in the way people claim some credit by saying they have been to the theatre or read a book or met a famous person. Familiarity with the

Bodleian, while not exactly arcane knowledge, is still in my mind a kind of rare privilege, as close to the sacraments as I will come.

The Bod, as the familiars call it (although academics refer to it simply as 'Bodley'), is made up of four buildings, the Radcliffe Camera, the Clarendon Building, the Old Bodleian, and the New Bodleian, the last routinely described as the ugliest building in Oxford.

In the thirties, to make way for the New Bodleian, three charmingly random houses were demolished in Broad Street. Gilbert Scott's building, wrote Jan Morris, looks like a municipal swimming bath. But the relationship between the old and the new is misleading: the New Bodleian is the coalface. There are eleven storeys of stacks, three of them below ground, and some miles of shelving – none of it normally open to the users – and even a small railway under Broad Street, where the Bodley Boys, intelligent but underprivileged lads, used to work until soon after the last war. The Bodley Boys were instituted by E.W.B. Nicholson, Chief Librarian. Nicholson was short on charm, but he was kind to the boys (and the few girls – he was something of a feminist) and took great pains to see that they were educated; many went on to take degrees at the university. At least two, now retired, are still working part-time in the library. They were paid 10s a week to move books on the railway from the New Bodleian, under Broad Street, to the Old Bodleian. Later the Boys and the pneumatic tubes were made redundant by a conveyor, which to this day delivers the books under the street and on to wherever they are needed in response to more than three hundred thousand requests a year.

To the east of the Old Schools Quadrangle, facing the main entrance to the Bodleian, is the great Gate and the Tower of the Five Orders built in honour of James I. The tower is decorated with the five orders of classical architecture, Doric, Tuscan, Ionic, Corinthian and Composite. The King presents a book to the university on which is written:

HAEC HABEO QUAE SCRIPSI.
HAEC HABEO QUAE DEDI

(These things I have which I have written. These things I have which I have given.)

Underneath the figure of James I is another inscription:

REGNANTE D. JACOBO REGUM
DOCTISSIMO MUNIFICENTISSIMO OPTIMO
HAE MUSIS EXTRUCTAE MOLES
CONGESTA BIBLIOTHECA ET
QUAECUNQUE ADHUC DEERANT AD
SPLENDOREM ACADEMIAE FELICITER
TENTATA COEPTA ABSOLUTA. SOLI DEO
GLORIA.

(In the reign of our godlike James, the most learned, generous and excellent of kings, these buildings were constructed for the service of the Muses, the library was assembled, and all that was still needed for the splendour of the university was happily planned, taken in hand, and completed. To God alone the glory.)

This is a building so grand that it is easy to imagine what was going on in the minds of the worthies of the university when, in 1623, they had it built as a tribute to the literary powers of James I. James is depicted giving his literary works to the university, under the caption 'Blessed be the Peacemakers'. Oxford is represented by a kneeling woman. Fame is blowing a trumpet in the direction of the King. What it tells us so obviously is how important the goodwill of the sovereign was to the university. James is also to be found on the gateway to Wadham College, standing above the founders. Only Cecil Rhodes, on the High Street frontage of Oriel, which he endowed, has a superior position to a king or queen on the billboard that is the entrance to many Oxford buildings. If you look closely at Rhodes, you will see that he is holding a bush hat in one hand. And if you look closely at most of the important buildings of Oxford, they can be seen to be semaphoring a message, not always edifying, of patronage and loyalty, which were often confused.

Just through the main entrance to the Bodleian Library is a kind of loggia, the Proscholium, and beyond that one of the most astonishing medieval buildings I have ever seen, the Old Divinity School, which acts as the support for Duke Humfrey's Library above. Duke Humfrey of Gloucester provided the first benefaction of books in the middle of the fifteenth century, about two hundred and fifty in all. The fan-vaulted ceiling, carved in stone in 1483, is truly a great work of British art. The ceiling, so my guide, William Clennell, retired librarian, tells me, is an exercise in power politics, linking the heraldic symbols and the monograms of many of the great benefactors and potentates of the time to form this miraculous reticule of stone. The royal coat of arms has pride of place, followed by that of Thomas Kemp, Bishop of London, the biggest donor, John Russell, and Henry Chichele, the founder of All Souls. There are four hundred and fifty-five carved bosses, each containing the coats of arms and initials of benefactors. There are other carved figures of the Virgin and Child over a crescent moon, and another of an eagle and child, which may have been the origin of the name of the famous pub where the literary group the Inklings used to meet, sometimes called the Bird and Baby. The whole building is miraculously light and airy, and the desks of the examiner and those being examined still stand there. Characteristically, I had never seen this ceiling until recently and I was unaware that, behind the Old Divinity School, is yet another wonderful building, the Convocation House, the university's parliament. During the Civil War, Charles I appropriated it for use as his parliament. It, too, has an astonishing fan-vaulted ceiling in stone, composed using medieval techniques. Beyond that is the chancellor's court, once used to control unruly undergraduates, fellows and loose women, and still retaining some limited powers.

Both these buildings, as well as Arts End in Duke Humfrey's library above, have been used in Harry Potter films and many others. As someone who once worked in the film business, I find the instinct of film people to discover and exploit beautiful buildings while at the same time being largely uninterested in any detail of their history or significance a particularly interesting and possibly a defining characteristic of our time. Duke Humfrey's Library, with its chained books in Arts End, is probably more recognisable now than it has ever been, thanks to Harry Potter. Up there Clennell has a surprise for me, my thesis deposited in 1970. It had been consulted twice in the intervening thirty-five years, once by P.E. Stephenson of Jesus in 1980, and once by David Tredinnick of St John's in 1987. Tredinnick is a former army officer and Conservative MP, with a reputation for being well to the right. Since then there has been a resounding lack of interest, although Clennell assured me that twice was twice more than most of them. For all its atmospheric charm, Duke Humfrey's has one of the world's greatest stores of ancient manuscripts. I remember finding bound within another book a small copy of Oliver Cromwell's tutor Thomas Beard's long – and justly – neglected work.

Over a couple of days Bill Clennell takes me all over the library. We start at the original library, the Old Library, in the university church of St Mary the Virgin used in the early fourteenth century. It is not a big room, about the size of a small church hall, and there is no sense that it was ever a library. One of its rules of those early days stated: '. . . that one of the two chaplains should inspect each who entered so that no one should go in with damp clothes, nor with pen and ink, nor with knife, but if he wished to extract anything from any book there he should only take with him tablets and a stile and so write what he wanted.' Now the books in Duke Humfrey's are alarmed. You are instructed to avoid placing anything on them or moving them without licence.

We move to James Gibbs's Radcliffe Camera, soaring vacantly upwards, the most profligate use of space in any library anywhere. Pevsner describes it as a 'totally splendid monumental waste of space of the whole centre'. When Hawksmoor's plan was finally put into effect in 1736, a number of houses were removed.

Since the re-design of 1969 the space has been used more effectively, but it still contains volumes of air.

We go on to the New Bodleian, the engine room of this great library. We see the Indian, Islamic and Hebraic collections and the Johnson Collection of Ephemera. This collection was made between the late-twenties and the mid-fifties by John Johnson, a printer and papyrologist: he described it as ‘a little museum of common printed things to illustrate at one and the same time our social life and the development of printing’. Categories include advertisements, artists, authors, bookbinders and publishers. Johnson also collected tickets, menus and greeting cards. One of the items is the playbill that George III was holding when he was shot. The result is powerfully evocative, because so much of it is an unmediated and naïve glimpse of a certain time. I often anyway find in unfamiliar cities that reading the small ads produces a great sense of the real life of these places: the desperate search for suitable wives by Indian graduates; offers of tuition in English in Africa; the variety of things that are commonly bought and sold – all these give one a feeling for everyday worries and anxieties. In

Johannesburg, for instance, there are hundreds of ads for guns and home-security systems, while at the same time there are ads for wildlife (a single zebra is only about £60) and borehole equipment. In this one juxtaposition you can see the longing for peace of mind and a rural idyll. And you can make what you will of the offers of massage parlours, warehouse religion and quick-fix education.

Down in the depths of the New Bodleian there is an enormous collection of children's books. Clennell asks me what I notice about them: they are remarkably clean, I say. Yes, the reason is that they are never taken out by children, simply kept as a record of books published. So first editions of *The Wind in the Willows*, *Treasure Island* and *Winnie the Pooh* sit serene and pristine on the shelves, never read, seldom requested, but fulfilling the function of a library of deposit. In addition to the deposits, the Bodleian acquires thousands of items a year from archives and bequests.

The Harding Collection of Printed Music is the bulkiest bequest the Bodleian has ever received. In 1974 it came from Chicago in a staggering nine hundred packing cases, the product of seventy years of collecting by Walton

N.H. Harding (1883–1973), who, although born in London, was a Chicagoan from the age of four. He had been one of the early ragtime pianists and collected song books, song sheets, British, French and American folk songs, as well as instrumental music and English music hall. In addition he collected broadside ballads, opera scores, poetry and drama and travel literature. He wanted this enormous collection to find a home in England, although he had never visited the Bodleian. The value of the collection is not so much in any single item, but in the comprehensiveness of its range. It includes a first edition of *Over the Rainbow*. The archive is now one of the most prized in the world for research into musical history and the library is heroically digitising it in response to this demand. Gazing at the boxes I am saddened by the knowledge that music is for me a dimly perceived hinterland. Isaiah Berlin loved music: he saw clearly that the effect music can have is not easily explained in rational terms, yet he understood at the same time that the feeling it engendered was real enough.

A few years ago I made a film about the Dead Sea Scrolls. The scrolls were being restored and preserved. For two thousand years

– probably since the Romans sacked Qumran in AD 70 – they had remained sealed in tall jars in the dry heat of caves above the Dead Sea. In the basement of the Rockefeller Museum in East Jerusalem, four Russian restorers, Jewish immigrants, were working on the scrolls painstakingly. Some of the larger scrolls are twenty-five feet long, including the Book of Isaiah, a complete version of Isaiah as we know it today, and the oldest-known Hebrew version of the Old Testament. These scrolls were part of the library of Qumran, copies of the Bible and commentaries, but recognisably arising from the same impulse as the one that created the Bodleian: the desire to cling to our culture, which has made us what we are.

The Book of Isaiah was brought into a room deep below the Rockefeller Museum and laid reverentially on a table for filming. The process was something like the scenes of unconscious and seriously ill patients being lifted carefully on to a trolley in *ER*. I found myself shaking; my knees were quite literally knocking, something I had imagined until that moment was simply a literary conceit.

> They shall beat their swords into ploughshares, and their spears into pruning hooks; nation shall not lift up sword against nation, neither shall they learn war any more.

Why, I wondered, was I so moved by this document? The most likely explanation is that these phrases have entered our culture and civilisation, and seeing them in their most ancient written form, much closer to the original impulse that brought them into being, was deeply moving. The idea of the Essenes labouring in this hell hole above the Dead Sea for two hundred years transcribing so diligently the books of their faith on to goat-skin parchment, along with their own interpretation of the prophet's words which – naturally – referred specifically to them and their estrangement from the Hasmonean priesthood in Jerusalem, suggested to me further evidence of something I have always believed, that it is in the act of writing that we attempt to moor ourselves in the unheeding universe. In my own writing life I find that I only know inchoately what I think until I have written it.

The Qumran community was relatively small, the life was hard and the sacrifices many, but the

Essenes persevered on this harsh hillside right up to the moment the Roman Tenth Legion destroyed their community. They just had time to hide the precious scrolls in the caves above the settlement, where they lay until 1947. The scrolls also give clues to an aspect of Judaism, and indeed of human nature, namely the unending disputatiousness. The Essenes believed they were the sons of righteousness and that those in charge of the Temple in Jerusalem were the sons of darkness. Life was a faltering progress towards absolute truth and only they were on the right path. In the final battle they would be victorious. This crazy idea that there is a single morality – essentially the view of all fundamentalists – has, we now see, not left the earth as rationalists expected it would. As Berlin put it: 'The world that we encounter in ordinary experience is one in which we are faced with choices between ends equally ultimate, and claims equally absolute, realisation of some of which must inevitably result in the sacrifice of others.' It might be the text for our times.

As I looked at the Book of Isaiah, I understood what the word 'numinous' really means: the *mysterium tremendum*, the overwhelming mystery, is not, I thought, anything to do with God, but a testament instead to the mystery of human striving; not, as the OED says, 'having a strong religious or spiritual quality: indicating or suggesting the presence of a deity'. No, it is the poignant, noble – and doomed – struggle of the human creature to make something permanent out of the meaningless and the ephemeral: out of mortality. The scrolls are beautifully and meticulously transcribed, but there are sometimes small corrections and omissions, which give them a human dimension. In Jerusalem, where I have travelled about eight times in all, I began to get the strange feeling that Roman and Judaic history of what is called the Common Era were not that long ago. The Discovery Channel producer of one of my films called me to complain that I was making too esoteric a point in the draft commentary: 'In America,' he said, 'some people think history is very old.' But I was at the time taking a different view: history seemed to me very present. The life of Jesus, for instance, acquires a new reality when you see the remains of Qumran from the central, ruined, tower, with the intentions of its people so clearly visible – the scriptorium, the refectory, the ritual baths and so on. This community predated Jesus by a hundred and fifty years, and lasted forty years after his death. Yet the documents the Essenes produced so painstakingly are wonderfully clear, and the biblical texts among them are almost exactly as in the Bible today. Until the scrolls were discovered, barely a scrap of papyrus or parchment had been found from that era.

I imagine that this feeling of domestic familiarity is what professional historians acquire almost without realising it as history loses its remoteness and acquires human nuances. In the Bodleian, when I read Adam von Trott's letters to Isaiah Berlin, the neat and beautiful handwriting, the occasional minor colloquial lapses, even the veiled hints about being in the opposition, seemed in the original to be especially potent and evocative. And when I was doing my thesis on Oliver Cromwell, I believed that I came to understand Cromwell's turn of phrase and religious imagery. Imagery seems to me to be highly revealing in unintended ways. In order to achieve the possibility of intimate understanding, we need some shared culture. And it is of course a truism that culture is partly founded on imagery – religious, nationalist, artistic. So two nations can live side by side in one country, yet rely on entirely different imagery for their understanding, as happened with the Cromwellians and the Royalists, and is the case now with many Muslims in Britain in relation to the non-Muslim population. If one is unsure about the essence of our culture, it is here in the Bodleian, outward-looking, interested, open-minded, not a closed system of belief or a set of unchanging propositions to be repeated ad nauseam. When I arrived here from South Africa, I felt myself liberated, and now, working in the Bodleian, I feel exactly the same exhilarating sense of possibility.

There is something in these seminal documents in the history of the progress of human thought – a progress that is incremental, and not necessarily in any prescribed direction – that I find ever more appealing, and that is the sense that a literate culture has the possibility of understanding other people's thoughts and ideas even if, as philosophers remind us, we can never fully understand another's mind. It may be that repetitive credos, which depend entirely on being faithful to some text as if it is the only explanation available, tell us a good deal about Islam, fundamental Judaism and literal Christianity.

In the Bodleian there are many documents of the greatest importance to Western culture.

Among these, I have chosen three of almost incomparable significance. The *Chanson de Roland* is the first great work of French literature, and the finest of the *chansons de geste*. The Oxford copy is, I was told, the sort of thing a *jongleur* might have carried in his pocket. It is indisputably the earliest authenticated copy of the *Chanson de Roland*. It came to Oxford in 1624 in the gift of Sir Kenelm Digby, whose tutor Thomas Allen had left him his papers. In the arcane way of libraries, it is known as Digby 23. It belongs to the last quarter of the twelfth century, and may have come to Oxford in the thirteenth century. The evidence for this is that it is bound with another book that was bequeathed to Osney Abbey in 1263. Now it has a kind of sacred status: as an Italian scholar describes it, there exists *un radicale misticismo verso il testo di O* (*testo di O* meaning the Oxford text). There are seven other manuscripts, three fragments and ten versions in other languages, but Oxford's, Digby 23, is the *ur-text*.

Dr Christopher Fletcher, Head of Western Manuscripts at the Bodleian, leads me to his office. It is high up beside the Tower of the Five Orders. We are some way below King James's knees. We look up to the King, like the supplicant woman who represents Oxford. On the wall near the window is a panel that reads: *Non Dormit Qui Custodit* that can be read as 'Curators should never sleep'. As a preamble Chris shows me some of the things that find their way weekly to the Bodleian: the Bodleian clearly has a magnetic attraction for those who wonder what to do with their treasures; I think that this glamorous appeal of Oxford is one of its greatest assets. Today a previously unknown letter from C.S. Lewis is waiting its rightful place. It is typed in fading blue ink. I long to read it, but I am all too aware that I am in here strictly under sufferance.

The Oxford *Roland* is so precious that it is kept in a vault in a secret location, I imagine somewhere in the building, but it seems like poor taste to enquire further: these are scholars, experts, to be treated with due delicacy. It is only now that I fully understand that what I am about to look at is rarely shown to any but the most serious scholars, about three or four per year; most people must make do with the digitised versions.

Waiting are two experts, Dr Bruce Barker-Benfield and Margaret Czepie, both curators of

Western manuscripts, who have the look of people who love what they do and could conceive of no better life than to be a curator of Western manuscripts in the Bodleian. At this moment, nor can I.

A box is unfastened, and there it is, at first sight a small red book. Dr Barker-Benfield opens the cover and points out the Digby family motto: *Vindicate te tibi*, which in my Latin has a Cosa Nostra-ish ring, something like a family mission statement, *Take care of business*. He points to the waste paper that has been used to pad out the binding, and then he shows me the book of astrological diagrams that are bound up with the Oxford *Roland*. These are a third-century Latin translation by Calcidius of Plato's *Timaeus*, copied in the twelfth century. Apparently any medieval scholar would have been familiar with the work. It is beautifully copied, but these meaninglessly elaborate designs of the planets and so on have as much appeal as medieval cosmology. But the great thing about the binding of the two books together is that it confirms that this is the oldest known copy, by at least forty years, of the *Chanson*. Dr Barker-Benfield points out that the *Roland* section is very worn. This suggests that, before the two sections were bound together in about 1283, the *Chanson* itself was much read and much handled. Its pre-1283 history can never be known, but it is quite possible because of its condition and its small size that it was a *jongleur*'s copy – a happy image – and almost certainly means that it was transcribed many years before it fetched up at Osney Abbey.

Unlike the Calcidius, it is not done by a professional scribe, merely the work of a competent academic – it is undoubtedly a copy – there are many small scribal errors. Experts put its date at somewhere between 1125 and 1140, so it is as close as we can get to the original of Turoldus, who probably wrote it in about 1100. A huge academic body of work is concerned with this little book: the nature of the *chanson de geste*, the relationship between the written words and the oral traditions of the *jongleurs*, the question of whether or not Roland was in some way culpable in the author's mind for the disaster of Roncevaux, the true understanding of the most famous line in the chanson – *Rollant est proz e Oliver est sage* – and much, much more, including the mathematics of the poetical construction. I am no expert, as people who rely on instinct rather than knowledge are fond of saying, but I incline towards the theory that *proz* meant worthy, not brave, so that this line proclaims that Roland and Olivier were both sensible, rather than that Roland was a foolhardy tearaway, in contrast to the solid Olivier, which has been the popular interpretation. These scholarly arguments are to me strangely cheering: I want to believe the world can accommodate scholars, not of the nineteenth-century type, who were so often trying to advance patriotic causes and arbitrary standards, nor scholars of the religious bigot variety, but scholars who try to understand other worlds and other minds. And here in the Bodleian, faced by one of the greatest artefacts of European culture, I again feel – without any justification whatever – somehow personally enriched.

Next, Margaret Czepie, who is a Pole, produces Kafka's draft of *The Castle*. In German *Schloss* can mean castle or lock. Although in the book the castle is not very impressive, I imagine that, from where Kafka lived in Old Town Square – 'in this little circle my whole life is contained' – the castle of Prague, huge, solid and forbidding, was an ever-present and overwhelming sight on the hill across the river, and more forbidding in fog: 'There was no sign of the castle hill, fog and darkness surrounded it,' as K approaches in the gloom.

I visited Prague Castle recently while writing a piece about a highly talented Czech boy, Petr Ginz, whose diaries and pictures have been published. He was interned at the age of fourteen in Terezin, and sent to his death in Auschwitz two years later. The castle seemed in its multiplicity of courtyards and entrances and doorways and mysterious passages to be a metonymy for what is now called Kafkaesque. Its many small windows, parade grounds and terraces look down, suspiciously, on the town; there is no mistaking its separateness from the town itself. And it is odd that Kafka has become the icon of Prague, when in fact he is the prophet crying out against totalitarianism, just as the emigration of Einstein, one of the icons of the new Berlin, was a warning of the Nazi horror to come. The upper classes of Prague spoke German. Charles University was founded in the fourteenth century, and was the first German-language university in Europe.

During the nineteenth century Czech was also used and until the war the university was divided into two sections. Kafka's family, like that of many prominent Jews, was German-speaking. It is one of the cruel ironies of the Nazi period that they should have destroyed the outposts of their own culture and particularly the German-speaking Jews outside Germany who adorned it. Marianne Steiner, Kafka's niece, who settled in England in 1938, was one of the few survivors of the family, and it was through her that the Kafka papers came to Oxford. Max Brod, Kafka's friend, who defied his wish that his papers should be destroyed, kept them in Tel Aviv after he emigrated to Palestine in 1938. Marianne Steiner recovered them by sheer persistence – various people, including Brod, had laid claim to them. Steiner gave the papers to the Bodleian, papers that include the manuscript of *The Castle*. It was untitled, but Brod said that was what Kafka intended to call the work.

South African literature, for obvious reasons, has been very heavily indebted to Kafka. Even the title of J.M. Coetzee's first Booker-winner, *The Life and Times of Michael K*, is a direct reference to Kafka. So to see this manuscript was particularly moving for me, although I think my state of mind can be attributed in part to a kind of provincial ambition, to get to the centre of things. I recently read an article on business tycoons who turned art collectors, and although the writer was scornful of their motives, I felt a certain sympathy: we are all trying in our own way to define ourselves, to mitigate our fate in the mortal world. Sometimes when I am speaking about books I use Samuel Beckett's line: 'Writing is not about something, it is that something,' but even as I say it I am aware there is an element of self-promotion in this kind of glib profundity. It is an unattractive trait of some writers only to claim familiarity with writers from the literary pantheon, and I suspect it springs from the same motive, of propelling oneself to the centre of things.

Researching the life of Petr Ginz, I had discovered a little of this lost German-speaking world. A visit to Terezin, where Petr Ginz was sent, revealed the full richness and range of talent of those the Nazis set out to destroy. *Brundibar*, colloquially a bumblebee in Czech, was Hans Krasa's children's opera, first performed by the children of Terezin. It had a libretto by Adolf Hoffmeister and became the symbol of the vital spirit that existed in Terezin, performed thirty or more times. Wonderful art and graphics were produced there. The German-speaking Jews of Prague were extraordinarily cultured and productive in literature, music and painting; this tradition was vigorously carried on in Terezin: Petr Ginz started a newspaper, wrote novels and drew marvellously well.

Young Ginz is survived by his sister Eva, and I have been in contact with her. She told me that the Ginz family was bilingual, although by the late-thirties Czech was favoured over German at home. There are apparently some distinctly Czech idioms in Kafka's German, which cannot be conveyed in the much debated English translations. Walking through Old Town Square to the Jewish school, the synagogues and on to the Ginz family apartment, followed by the long ascent to the castle, I couldn't but see Kafka's world. If Prague has become a cheery tourist backdrop, Terezin thirty miles away, where Ginz was sent at fourteen, still presents a truly Kafkaesque front to the world. What W.G. Sebald noticed in his book *Austerlitz*, the awful dull wariness of the place, almost chokes the visitor. The fortified town, built for eight thousand soldiers, once held sixty thousand of Europe's most distinguished Jews, most of them murdered in Auschwitz. Now it has only a few furtive residents. Deserted parade grounds, a never-open antique shop, two cafés and a couple of museums welcome the trickle of tourists. This is one of the most unsettling places I have ever been. It is certainly the most Kafkaesque. Ottla, Kafka's favourite sister, was transported here, as were Ginz and his sister Eva. She told me that after the Russians liberated her from Terezin, she arrived home with her father, and her waiting mother's first question was, 'Where is Petr?' She did not know, although Terezin is so close to Prague, that Petr and his cousin and uncle had been sent to Auschwitz a year before. The rail lines of the siding from where they were transported are still visible in Terezin. And those rail lines, which I photographed, seemed to have been prefigured by Kafka. I must add, with some pride, that Eva wrote to me to tell me that my piece was the best and most perceptive of the many written about her brother.

The Castle was first published by Max Brod two years after Kakfa's death in 1924. Brod made a number of changes – which he explains in his introduction – of punctuation, spelling and even the order of words and chapters. He omitted the last few pages. When the Kafka papers came to Oxford in 1961, Malcolm Pasley and his colleagues began a new edition of

The Castle which restored many of Kafka's idiosyncrasies and eliminated many of the mistakes of the earlier editions. Pasley himself made some changes; now a facsimile edition of the manuscript is available. To see the excisions and corrections for myself, and to see the last page broken off in mid-sentence is truly astonishing: *aber was sie sagte* . . . Brod said that his friend never intended it to be unfinished, and explained that he had cut the last few pages because they were leading to a new, and unfinished twist in the story. The manuscript is written in ink in six soft-cover notebooks, probably – Margaret Czepie thinks – just standard school exercise books. Kafka's handwriting reminds me of von Trott's.

Brod's view of Kafka was largely accepted for years. Brod was, after all, Kafka's friend and – twice – saviour of his work from oblivion. The Muirs, who first translated *The Castle*, included Brod's own foreword, and they were deeply influenced by his interpretation of Kafka as a religious genius in an age of scepticism: the village and the castle represent a religious society to which K aspires hopelessly. It's hardly surprising that the rise of Nazism has given the book so much added significance. But Brod, and therefore the English translators, seemed to have discounted what J.M. Coetzee has tellingly described as Kafka's understanding of 'the obscene intimacies of power'. Nonetheless it is true that Kafka was the classic outsider, thwarted in his longing for marriage, often ill, never able to accept the love of his family or women. Still, he is not easily contained within his friend Brod's religious view of him. So the Oxford manuscript of *The Castle* is not merely a thing of wonder, but also offers years of intrigue and dispute, which, of course, would have a wonderful Kafkaesque symmetry if no resolution can ever be achieved.

From his tower room, Chris Fletcher leads me to the New Bodleian across Broad Street. Clive Hurst is waiting in a fine room, one of the few untouched rooms of the New Bodleian. The exterior may look like a municipal swimming bath, but in here there is a kind of confident solidity, characteristic of inter-war architecture. Hurst is the keeper of Oxford's Shakespeare First Folio, and Head of Rare Books. There are still two hundred and forty-seven First Folios of the original run of seven hundred and fifty, so this is far from the rarest manuscript in the world. But it can be shown to be the oldest still in its original binding. Bindings, I am learning, are the palaeontology of archivists. First Folios may not be rare, but they have been subject to a powerful and quasi-religious movement of what has been called 'bardolatory'. The Folger Shakespeare Library in Washington DC has seventy-nine copies; Henry Clay Folger, its founder, established his museum in 1930 right at the centre of Washington life, as if to suggest a sort of national spiritual link with the Bard. He had been deeply affected in the middle of the nineteenth century by a lecture given on the Bard at Amherst, where he was a student, by Emerson.

The First Folio was collected by Shakespeare's actor colleagues John Hemminge and Henry Condell in 1623, seven years after Shakespeare's death: thirty-six plays in all, eighteen of which had never been published before. Some were in Shakespeare's own hand. In their preface Hemminge and Condell regret that Shakespeare is not alive to help them: the plays came from many kinds of sources, and in very different states of accuracy; some were based on actors' memories, which are regarded as 'bad quartos'; there are author's early drafts for actors – 'foul papers' –

and fair but unreliable copies from professional scribes, commissioned by the editors. The First Folio runs to over seven hundred pages.

Clive Hurst opens the tooled box that contains Oxford's First Folio. *Mr WILLIAM SHAKEPEARES COMEDIES, HISTORIES, & TRAGEDIES. Publifhed according to the True Originall Copies* is there, decorated with Martin Droeshut's famous, if rather odd, engraving. Shakespeare looks faintly alarmed.

Why, I ask, is it special? Clive Hurst explains that it was received in 1623 by the Bodleian under the terms of their agreement with the Stationer's Company in loose sheets. It was bound in 1624 by William Wildgoose and entered into the library's catalogue. It was chained in Arts End until about 1664, when it was replaced by a copy of the Third Folio, which contained another twelve plays. It was sold, the records suggest, in a group of superfluous books to Richard Davis, Oxford bookseller, for £24. In 1905 Gladwynn Turbutt, a Magdalen man, came to Oxford with a First Folio, wanting to know what to do with it. Because of the brown calf binding and the waste paper that lines the binding, identical to other paper Wildgoose used at the time, and because of the marks where the chains had been attached to the binding, it was quickly identified as the very same copy the library had once owned. Now the young man decided to sell: Henry C. Folger offered £3,000, a huge amount for a manuscript at the time. Up until then the library's record bid had been £220 10s. for a collection of Anglo-Saxon documents. Turbutt said that the Bodleian could have the First Folio if they could match Turbutt's offer within a week. In fact it took some months, and required a begging letter in *The Times* from E.W.B. Nicholson – of Bodley Boys fame – to winkle the last five hundred out of Lord Strathcona. Nicholson wrote:

> That after two and a half centuries we should have the extraordinary chance of recovering this volume, and lose it because a single American can spare more money than all Oxford's sons and friends who have been helping us, is a bitter prospect. It is the more bitter because the abnormal value put on this copy by our competitor rests on knowledge ultimately derived from our own staff and our own registers. But from so cruel a gibe of fortune this appeal may perhaps yet spare us.

Lord Strathcona's money was received two days before the extended deadline.

Clive Hurst shows me the papers that line the bindings. He says that judging by the wear and tear, *Romeo and Juliet*, particularly the balcony scene, was the most read play, followed by *Julius Caesar* and *The Tempest*. Least popular with the graduates (no undergraduates were allowed in Duke Humfrey's) were *King John* and *Richard II*. It is intriguing to wonder what it was that appealed in the balcony scene. Was it because it was about the young men's own generation, or was it as a text most studied, or did it have a certain erotic appeal? Were the students who thumbed it for forty years reading it for pleasure, or under compulsion?

Incidentally, there is in Oxford's St Aldate's a secretarial services agency, located in a room that was once apparently part of the Crown Inn where Shakespeare spent nights on his way to and from Stratford. He was a friend of the landlord. The dull panelling in this dingy office is rolled back, and there are the original walls, richly, even gaudily, decorated in the style of the late sixteenth century. This fragment of a Tudor inn would almost certainly be a major tourist attraction if it were advertised; instead it has a dual role as a dreary provincial office and a secret cultural shrine, oddly furtive. Bardolatory has barely reached this nook just between Prêt à Manger and Boots.

So Oxford's First Folio has a clearly authenticated history; the two actors who assembled this from 'the true originall copies' – a blatant lie – did the world an incalculable service: the First Folio established Shakespeare's enduring reputation. But it proved for the tyro publishers a very difficult task. Some of the sources were poor, and two plays, *Love's Labours Won* and *Cardenio*, were never found; *Pericles*, not included in F1, exists only in a very unreliable form; some of the original copies Hemminge and Condell acquired were in Shakespeare's own hand, and many had elaborate notes and even new pages inserted. Hemminge and Condell claim that Shakespeare's 'mind and hand went together, and what he thought and he uttered with that easiness we have scarce received from him a blot on his papers' is another lie. As for Droeshut's engraving, it may have been done from a lost portrait: as a likeness it is far from conclusive, although Francis Bacon was prevailed upon by the editors to claim it was a true portrayal. The dedications are contradictory: one assures the Earls of Montgomery and Pembroke that the Folio's very existence is thanks entirely to their patronage, while a second tells 'the Great Variety of Readers' that it is a commercial venture, entirely dependent on their support. They urge them to buy.

When the copies were finally ready in 1624, they sold for 15s. unbound and £1 in calf. The fetishisation of Shakespeare objects means that a First Folio now sells for millions. The Oriel First Folio was sold in 2003 for £2.8 million and recently a very fine copy, once owned by John Dryden's niece, sold for $6,166,000, at that time £4,166,216. As Michael Dobson writes in the *Guardian*, this is a terrific amount of money for a not-very-rare manuscript. He also wonders why the Japanese should collect the F1. There are fifteen in Japan. His conclusion is that during the eighteenth century 'this sublimely useless commodity' became a fetish object. But I think he perhaps underestimates the mythopoeic qualities of anything related to Shakespeare, even of a rather suspect edition of thirty-six plays published well after his death. In a world where rich people can own any number of Picassos, planes, houses and racehorses, and endow any number of hospitals and colleges and museums, there is – to me anyway – a perfectly understandable tendency to want something so central to our cultural identity, even if there are two hundred and forty-eight more of them out there. It is in the nature of great wealth – and in this respect it is not all that different from more modest human aspirations – to try to validate itself. How can you do this more effectively than by associating yourself intimately with Shakespeare? The cynical might say by reading Shakespeare, but that might be asking too much of the wealthy – money keeps them very busy.

Talking to Clive Hurst, I realise that this F1, with its long connections to Oxford, is, in his view, the most important single manuscript in the Bodleian. I ask him if he feels a certain proprietorship: he does, although he knows that his dominion is for a limited period of time. And I see again something that struck me at the beginning: Oxford is just the setting, the location – as they say in films – against which this pageant is played eagerly by successive generations. And I wonder too, as I walk out into a bright autumn afternoon, if I have not been guilty of failing to see the obvious, that Oxford has a kind of wildly enhanced significance for me because I was young and almost ecstatically happy here, and I think that I am guilty also of believing it has added lustre to my life, a kind of imagined distinction, which has more to do with my upbringing and origins than any reality.

On a whim I walk under the Bridge of Sighs and into New College Lane. A few summers ago I went to see *The Tempest*, one of the seventeenth-century students' favourites, performed in the cloisters. But this lane looks strangely unfamiliar, the stone dark and uncleaned, the walls blank, windows blocked up, and even some sixties graffiti on a stone window frame. I experience a few moments of profound disorientation. Clearly New College must be to the left, but I can't ever remember walking down here, nor do I recognise the strange barn-like building that lines the lane. It is like Kafka's castle, blank and mysterious. A Georgian house stands curiously walled off. Eventually I pass St Edmund's Hall and arrive at the High Street, having gone through almost one hundred and eighty degrees. I wonder if I haven't latched on to this Oxford stuff – as my wife sometimes suggests of me – a pilot fish sucking up to a whale, a colonial trying to make himself more cosmopolitan by association. A fraud on the verge of exposure. I walk up the stream-like windings of that glorious street – as Wordsworth described the High. I cheer myself up with the sheer pleasure of walking these streets, of feeling them under my feet, of hearing bells break out. Now I turn down Magpie Lane and head for Christ Church Meadow, so different from New College Lane, light and open and rural. The rugby fields are unused, but they are ready in the bright autumn chill. I remember so well that strange excitement, a nervous excitement, before a match, the lines painted, the grass a rich green, the beautiful but faintly menacing feel of a rugby field. A man sits in his shirtsleeves with his back against a wall drinking something from a cup, underneath a sign that reads 'Keep off the Grass'. I imagine something truculently non-conformist about him: not wearing enough clothes when it is cold can be a sign of mental disorder. In the Memorial Gardens, awed by the majesty of Christ Church behind, strung with red and gold Virginia creeper, I see a single enormous white nicotiana in full flower. Now I have turned back into the High and head up to the Radcliffe Camera. I have gone through more than three hundred and sixty degrees; in fact I am going round in circles, which may have some symbolism. I remember Isaiah Berlin's claim that this is the most beautiful square in Europe. In his last known essay Berlin described true knowledge as the knowledge of why we are what we are. I imagine that he was conscious of how he had got to where he found himself. I hope that in a way I share his appreciation of this place for the same reason, that we both came from somewhere else and were allowed, even encouraged, to become part of it.

5

Some time ago it struck me that museums tell you as much about the age in which they were founded as they do about their ostensible purpose. T.S. Eliot said of art that each generation takes from it what it requires. And I think you can apply that observation with justice to museums.

Oxford has four major museums, the Ashmolean on Beaumont Street, which is the university museum of art and archaeology, now being completely reorganised at the cost of some millions, the University Museum of Natural History on Parks Road, the Museum of the History of Science, on Broad Street, and the Pitt-Rivers Museum, next to and conjoined with the Natural History Museum. The Pitt-Rivers has also been reorganised and in the near future will be opened up to the Natural History Museum to reveal the airiness of the original design. I have absolutely no recollection of visiting any of them when I was a student.

On the way to and from my digs in Chalfont Road in that area of North Oxford that John Betjeman loved, an area of tall Victorian villas and neatly laid-out streets, I would walk past the Natural History Museum with my friend Hugh Williams, now a television man, the brother of Nigel Williams the writer, also a friend. We would invent long comic dialogues, which went on for days. One of these involved a Jewish frankfurter manufacturer in the Bronx, and we would do the accents as the father implored the son not to go to Princeton but to enter the business. Hilarious, as I recall.

I find myself increasingly envious, even jealous, of the young, whose lives are punctuated by ecstasy as mine was then. People talk of happiness as though it is the absence of anything too oppressive or unpleasant – bereavement, or illness or debt – but actually the happiness of youth is blitheness, the sheer physical joy of being young and beautiful, of living in your skin, aware, but only theoretically, of what lies ahead, without the concomitant responsibilities. I recognise in one of my sons – who was at Oxford – an almost frantic desire to keep intact the camaraderie and happiness of Oxford, to escape – although he knows it is impossible now that he is in the world – the petty and the major responsibilities to come. At Oxford you have an identity that is self-evident: you have been admitted to a charmed life, to the intimacy and fellowship of what, let's be candid, is a privileged life and one that can never be fully remade. I remember one summer, spent in Rome with Oxford friends working on Nevill Coghill's film, *Dr Faustus*, thinking that I would never be this happy again. Even then the realisation was painful. And a very recent graduate told me of her pain on going back to Oxford, wanting to re-create the life, but realising that it had gone for ever.

To reach the Pitt-Rivers, you have to pass through the Natural History Museum. This is an eccentric arrangement, as they are separate entities. The Natural History Museum is an extraordinary building. Flying upwards, a marvel of the new mastery of iron and glass, it looks like a highly cerebral railway station, the columns decorated with acanthus and fruits and supported by great blocks of British stone. Around the walls of the building is a mezzanine floor, from which you can lock on to the gaze of giant dinosaur skeletons, including an iguanodon. The reconstruction shows the iguanodon as having enormous claws. Once it was thought to have a horn on its nose, but later finds showed that this horn was in fact a tooth. Not only that, but the iguanodon was not a biped as earlier reconstructions suggested.

This central hall is designed to tell the story of human life and its rise from the mud. It also contains the famous dodo, or what is left of it. In fact the original dodo became mouldy and was burned, but a foot and the beak are still on display and a reconstruction stands near by. The dodo is at least as famous as Charles Dodgson's inspiration for its role in *Alices's Adventures in Wonderland* as it is for being extinct. Dodgson, who stammered, referred to himself as Do-do-Dodgson. The model for Alice was the daughter of the Dean of Christ Church, a potentate of the university and the Lord of Christ Church. He is responsible for the magnificent avenue of trees leading down to the river, planted as a triumphal way for the heroes of the newly fashionable sport of rowing. The Dean's garden, Alice's garden, can be visited only through specialist tours.

In another display in the Natural History

Museum, a white rabbit and a little owl and a tortoise are grouped to remind the viewers of Dodgson's astonishing imagination: 'We call him tortoise because he taught us.' (This rhyme doesn't quite work with the ever more popular pronunciation 'tortoys'.) Penelope Lively described Dodgson to me as the first children's writer to write about the arcane and incomprehensible adult world from a childish perspective. She was also quite dismissive of the idea that he might have been a paedophile. At that time it was considered natural for the dons, who were all celibate, to seek the company of young friends. Alice Liddell, the Dean of Christ Church's daughter, was photographed by Dodgson, and I think it has to be said that the pictures have a consciously erotic content, but it may be that even a degree of eroticism was considered charming rather than sinister. The mysterious rift with the Liddell family, and the removal after his death in 1898 of some pages from Dodgson's diary referring to the key years 1858–1862, have added to the suspicions. A later note by Alice's brother says that Dodgson was paying too much attention to the nursemaid and to the older sister, but this may have been a diversion. Whatever the truth of the suspicions, there is no doubt at all that Dodgson's fantastic world, grounded in Oxford, but graced by his extraordinary understanding of logic, mathematics, poetics and the minds of children, is a work of genius. And as with many great literary works, Oxford has to some extent defined itself in accordance with Dodgson's world.

It was in a room of the Natural History Museum that the famous encounter, which subsequent retelling turned into a legend, took place between the Bishop of Oxford, Samuel 'Soapy Sam' Wilberforce, and T.H. Huxley, Darwin's Bulldog, on 30 June 1860. Wilberforce asked Huxley whether it was on his grandfather's or his grandmother's side that he was descended from an ape. Huxley replied that if he were given the choice of being descended from an ape or from someone who used his intellect simply to introduce ridicule into a grave scientific discussion, 'I would unhesitatingly affirm my preference for the ape.' The more popular, but inaccurate, version of the exchange is this: 'Is it on your grandfather's or grandmother's side that you claim descent from the apes?' to which Huxley replied: 'I would rather be descended from an ape than a bishop.' Huxley's riposte, although devastating, was delivered very quietly, and not heard by all present. There are a number of accounts of the confrontation, one of which suggests that the high tension of it all caused ladies to faint.

In a letter to Darwin, Joseph Hooker, who was present at the debate, claimed that it was he who had saved the day for the cause, because Huxley had spoken too politely. Huxley decided after that evening to improve his debating skills in the cause of science, which he did. As with most epochal encounters, the myth runs a little ahead of the facts. Wilberforce, after a long and tedious lecture given by a Professor Draper of New York University, was probably simply trying, misguidedly, to liven up the evening. He had himself written a review of Darwin's *Origin of Species* that demonstrated that he was no heedless opponent of science:

> We have no sympathy with those who object to any facts or alleged facts in nature, or to any inference logically deduced from them, because they believe them to contradict what it appears to them is taught by Revelation. We think that all such objections savour of a timidity which is really inconsistent with a firm and well-intrusted faith.

Darwin himself acknowledged that Wilberforce had made some strong points in his review of *Origin of Species*.

So Wilberforce was not the religious bigot and sneering oaf that legend has made him. For all that, this was the decisive moment when the scientists and rationalists took hold of the great debate. The rather confused exchange was seen by a substantial minority as the tipping point, when religion could no longer dictate to science the legitimate areas of discussion nor dictate what the ultimate truths were. From that moment it was widely understood that the ends of religion and science were irreconcilable. Oxford itself was about to shake off the old beliefs, and its recognisable modern character began to emerge. The rearguard action of the Tractarians and the Ruskinites was doomed, just as the day of the clergyman-dons was closing. Soon it would be ridiculous to proclaim, as they did in the first half of the century: 'There is one province of education indeed in which we are slow in believing that any discoveries can be made. The scheme of revelation we think is closed, and we expect no new light on earth to break in upon us.'

Alice's Adventures in Wonderland was published just a few years after the famous debate.

Oxford was then deep in the convulsions of the Oxford Movement, transfixed by the realisation that science had been neglected and wracked by reforms in the way undergraduates were taught, reforms encouraged by Gladstone in the eighteen seventies. Gladstone also acted to remove the requirement that dons should give a declaration of religious faith. Keble College, named after John Keble, the father of the Oxford Movement, was founded in 1870, and stands opposite the Natural History Museum. Beatrix Potter thought that it looked like a building from a London suburb. In 1930 Christopher Hobhouse was still able to say it was 'violently offensive to all senses . . . the colours and proportions can only be described as obscene'. Now, in all its splendour, it stands boldly in the sunshine when, as Hugh Casson writes, its 'brickwork, hot in colour, and warm to the touch, flickers and glows'. But its symbolic purpose was clear. Edward Pusey wrote: 'Keble lies as it were to give a broadside for Christianity to the Museum.' The college may have been founded to counter the atheistic possibilities of science, but it was also determinedly anti-aristocratic. Its architect, William Butterfield, wanted it to look unlike any other, traditional, college for this reason, and in this he succeeded. Strange that both Keble and the Natural History Museum should have adopted what were then uncompromisingly modern designs, one a mock Gothic cathedral of science, the other a riot of highly controversial coloured brick.

The Light of the World, finished by William Holman Hunt in 1853, was donated to the college, soon after its foundation in 1870, by the widow of Thomas Combe, who bought it for 400 guineas; it hangs in a side chapel, which was built expressly to house it after Butterfield rejected it as too small for the main chapel. It is an astonishing picture, but not a truly great picture because of its mawkishness. Ruskin, however, thought it was 'one of the very noblest works of sacred art ever produced in this or any other age'. It can be seen, at certain times every week, proclaiming the light of the world. As you enter the side chapel, still blinded by the ferocious confidence of the enormous chapel, you press a simple switch to illuminate the picture. Having seen it a hundred times in facsimile, I found that it was indeed small, but loaded with biblical significance. Its inspiration is a passage in Revelation: 'Behold, I stand at the door, I will come to him and will sup with him, and he with me.' It was common then to believe that every fact and every event in the Bible bears some meaning if we can only winkle it out: we must separate the physical and the spiritual. (Dualism was a philosophical favourite of the time.) Holman Hunt went to great lengths to make what was to be considered his masterpiece. He had a version made of the lantern that Christ is holding, and spent long hours studying the effects of light from this lantern on moonlight nights. Often he would paint from 2 a.m. until first light. The crown, cloak and robes that Christ is wearing also bear volumes of meaning: the cloak is intended to evoke kingship and the high priesthood, the jewelled clasp on the cloak indicates righteousness, the trees behind prefigure crucifixion, and the crown and aureole around Christ's head indicate his divinity. The lamp on which Holman Hunt spent so much time was a reference to the Psalms: 'The word is a lamp unto my feet and a light unto my path.' But the lamp was not his only concern. In a room of his house he built a small set: 'I had made up an imitation door . . . and had placed a long figure for the drapery, with the lantern to shine upon dimly; in the day I could screen out the sun, and at night I removed the blinds to let in the moon.'

Lizzie Siddal modelled for the hair, and Hunt may have used a male figure for the head, but if he did, his identity was kept secret. Thomas Carlyle had a preview of the painting. He was scathing:

> . . . empty make-believe, mere pretended fancy, the like of which is the worst of occupations for a man to take on. Do you ever suppose that Jesus walked about bedizened in priestly robes and a crown with yon jewels on his breast and a gilt aureole round his head?

The painting caused a sensation when it was first exhibited. Its hyperrealism was glamorous and it contained a very modern knowingness about public taste. William Bell Scott wrote: 'For the first time in this country a picture became a subject of conversation and general interest from one end of the island to the other, and indeed continued so for many years.' During its first exhibition the marriage of John and Effie Ruskin was dissolved. Millais, who married Effie, wrote in some detail to Hunt, both about this fact and about the reception the painting had had.

So popular was it, that Holman Hunt painted a life-sized version, which hangs to this day in St Paul's Cathedral. This painting toured the world, even reaching Australia, where fifteen thousand saw it in the National Gallery of Victoria alone. There are two strange facts about this copy: one, that Hunt was blind when it was painted and, two, that it was never taken down from St Paul's during the Second World War.

Although by the time the painting was hung in its special side chapel in 1895 the Anglo-Catholic movement at Oxford had lost ground, its final resting place is appropriate. Keble's chapel commemorates the college's spiritual progenitors, Pusey, Wilberforce, Liddon, Beachamp, King and Newman; Keble and the painting can be seen as the last trumpet of their ideas about the paramount importance of religion in the world. So it also, in a sense, marks the start of the modern age of Oxford, or at least an Oxford I recognise. This extraordinarily charged time, with university reform in full flood, Darwinism on the rise, religious feeling running high, science belatedly receiving its due, can be seen, I think, as the cauldron out of which modern Oxford was made. The removal of religious qualifications, the reforms of the colleges, the rise of the dons, including those who were to produce liberal-intellectual dynasties, led to the heyday of the dons, which lasted, according to Noel Annan, until the seventies, when dons began to lose influence in the world. And it is true that when I was at Oxford there were many dons who were public figures: Berlin foremost, but also A.J. Ayer, Maurice Bowra, Hugh Trevor-Roper, A.L. Rowse, E.H. Carr and many of Harold Wilson's cabinet, including Patrick Gordon Walker and Richard Crossman. Now Richard Dawkins is probably the only figure a large number outside Oxford have heard of.

As I look at the dodo and the dinosaurs and *The Light of the World*, and as I think about *Alice's Adventures*, I see for the first time how they are all connected, and I realise that, as I get older, I am becoming increasingly interested in these connections, as if human life is indeed a web, and one small event or idea can send tremors to the outer perimeter. What happens beyond the outer perimeter, where we are all headed, is of no interest, because nothing we imagine beyond blankness makes sense.

In the museum I hear a conversation that could only have taken place in Oxford: I hear a woman saying, reasonably but firmly, 'No, you look at them and then you tell me. Look at them closely.' I don't hear the reply, but I turn round and see that the woman is talking to a child of no more than two years old, who is sitting in a pushchair: 'That's right, fish. It's a group of fossil fish.' And there they are, not all that easy to discern, fish that have left their shapes in limestone some millions of years ago.

The Pitt-Rivers Museum was added to the Natural History Museum in order to house the collection of Lieutenant General Augustus Henry Lane-Fox Pitt-Rivers. He gave twenty thousand objects to the university in 1896 on two conditions, that a special museum be built and that a lecturer in anthropology be appointed. Behind his enthusiasm for collecting was a very Victorian idea, that these artefacts would demonstrate a progression in the design and the evolution of human culture, towards the more complex. It would be a museum casting light on the most important subject, the story of humankind. But as the museum's brochure reads: 'These ideas are no longer accepted and today the displays celebrate cultural diversity.' There is something in that word 'celebrate' that suggests to me a certain hypocrisy. Poor old Pitt-Rivers had wanted to show, despite Conrad and others, that evolution was going somewhere – upwards – but he ended up demonstrating only that different cultures have similar ways of doing things. Lévi-Strauss believed that people use whatever means are at hand to survive and they apply whatever beliefs they can to fix their moral position. But cultural diversity, as is obvious, is not always and for ever something to celebrate. It may be something to admire or to ponder, which is a different proposition altogether. For example, is the Pitt-Rivers celebrating clitoridectomy and boiled skulls and suttee?

In college prospectuses mom-and-apple-pie phrases are creeping in, about health and safety and sexual diversity, which seem to me to be strangely hollow. In Trinity the President of the JCR told me that she had two officers dealing with the problems of sexual diversity. When I told her that in my day the main job of the President of the JCR was to get the beer in – it was Alastair Sawday of the eponymous travel guides – I saw that she thought of me as antediluvian; in fact just like one of my characters in

The Promise of Happiness, I was being deliberately and counter-productively provocative. I have found that when I am writing I can become so deeply involved with individual characters – but not all of them – that I begin to ape them. John Updike told me that he is slightly mystified by my belief that Harry 'Rabbit' Angstrom is one of the great creations of American literature. When he started the series, back in 1969, he had no idea that it would be a series at all, and also he thought Rabbit was very unlikeable. But it is clear that literature takes no account of likeable or unlikeable in making its judgements, and Rabbit is one of the most fully alive characters in twentieth-century fiction. I also see clearly that Rabbit contains a good deal of Updike, in his essentially patriotic and hopeful nature and his high sensitivity to women.

As I wander around the Pitt-Rivers I find something extraordinary: in the main hall, a wonderfully cluttered place full of cabinets and display cases, with canoes and outriggers hanging from the roof, I see a collection of Haida doorposts from British Columbia that once stood at the entrances to communal houses on Queen Charlotte's Island. And while I was in Vancouver just a few weeks before, I saw exactly these in the wonderful Museum of Anthropology there, which is largely devoted to the life and work of the Haida, a remarkable people. In the strange jumble of the Pitt-Rivers, alongside 'Treatment of the Dead' and 'Feathers and Beadwork', these astonishing totems rise two floors upwards. Of course, as with all ethnography, things change: they are not properly totem poles (the corruption of a Great Lakes term) but crest poles. In Vancouver they are set in a beautiful and purpose-built museum and earnest guides tell you the whole uplifting story of the native peoples, ecologists, who cropped whales and trees sensitively and lived utterly irreproachable lives. Here in Oxford these astonishing objects, 11.36 metres high, made of Canadian Red Cedar, are virtually anonymous. The crests of each family are represented by symbolic animals: a bear, with a cub between its legs, eats a frog. Another bear with two bear cubs at its feet holds a human baby. The crest poles were carved to mark a *potlash*, the granting of family rights through the exchange of gifts. I also find Crow and Ojibwa clothing, with the strange French-influenced flower patterns, which I instantly recognise from some research I once did for a novel.

(Novelists often have magpie tendencies.) And over at the Ashmolean Museum is the ceremonial cloak of Powhatan, the father of Pocahontas, who is buried in Gravesend. This beautiful, priceless and poignant object made of deerskin and shells will, I am sure, receive its due when the Ashmolean is re-organised. The Ashmolean takes its name from Elias Ashmole, a seventeenth-century collector, who was given by John Tradescant his extraordinary collection of 'peculiars', which formed the basis of Oxford's first museum, and included Powhatan's Mantle and Oliver Cromwell's death mask. As I write this, the Ashmolean's exterior has emerged, refreshed, in beautiful pale colours, and work is under way on the interior.

Perversely, I hope the Pitt-Rivers never changes its amateur-collector appearance. These handwritten labels, the antiquated cataloguing, the treasure accessible only to people who know what they are looking for, all this appeals to me, and has done to many other people including James Fenton, the poet, and Penelope Lively, both of whom have written about it.

In a small room at the Pitt-Rivers a film about Frederick Spencer Chapman's expedition to Lhasa in 1936 is running. Thousands of horsemen wheel in homage to the Dalai Lama. Richard Gere's birth is seven years away, and while the idea that people in remote corners of the earth have secrets has reached Oxford, the news that these secrets are expressly designed to transform the lives of the rich in Beverly Hills has not yet arrived. Penelope Lively told me of the genesis of her classic, *The House in Norham Gardens:* she was thinking of a way of introducing the concept of death in a children's book, and the Pitt-Rivers, with its slightly strange and eerie atmosphere, provided the answer. The young heroine, Claire, discovers a wooden head in the attic of the house and this leads her to the Pitt-Rivers. She also said something I found interesting, if alien: her relationship with Oxford was not passionate; although Oxford has played a great part in her life, she is not nostalgic about it. Perhaps, she thought, because so many hundreds of thousands have passed through, it has a huge collective imagination, and so she could not feel a personal response: private places are more intimate, and mean more to her. And later I wondered – at the risk of oversimplifying – about whether there isn't something in the sexes that produces a different response to place, the female response being much more tuned to the personal and domestic. She remembered her first child being born at the Radcliffe with great vividness, and her favourite places, like the Parks and the Pitt-Rivers, are associated with her children. She also described being interviewed by Iris Murdoch for a place at St Anne's. Iris was lying on the floor, and asked her what she was reading on the train up to Oxford. She was being interviewed for a place to read history, but Iris suggested PPE instead. I asked Penelope about the famous relationship between dons and crime novels: her husband, Jack, loved crime novels, she said. She thought that for clever people it was simply a way of switching off, a sort of minor diversion like the crossword. I think that sport plays this role for many less intellectual men: the closed system, each game with a result, each game ritualised, repetitive, almost meaningless on a day-to-day level, and each one involving emotions that are not very deep and loyalties that are not very dangerous. I have occasionally been to the Arsenal and listened to the crowd screaming at the referee and the opposition players, with a hatred and venom that bordered on the irrational, and a level of obscenity that was strangely disturbing. The very spiritual James Helmuth von Moltke, one of those Germans hanged by Hitler, suggested that a nation needs a war once in a while to clear the air. Or to put it less dramatically, a nation needs some bigger issues: the Iraq War, curiously, seems to me the sort of issue that we should not be involved in, precisely because it only involves, on our side, a very small section of the population, with the rest of us jeering from the sidelines while thousands die.

The Pitt-Rivers now has a magnificient new wing to house the staff – some of whom previously had to sit in a gloomy corridor – a research library and other facilities. I was there in 2007 when it was declared open by my friend Michael Palin. Yet the musuem still represents aspects of Oxford that I find attractive: disinterested pursuit of knowledge, an indifference to modishness – not the same thing as being insensitive to it – a respect for the ethos of its benefactor – itself worth study – and a kind of domesticity. It is this domesticity that I ponder as I walk through the Parks. The fact that T.E. Lawrence lived at 2 Polstead Road amazed me when I came to Oxford. And the homeliness of Iffley Road seemed too minor for the location of the first sub-four-minute mile, by a medical student. It was as if a kind of amateur enthusiasm and bags of confidence were all that was required to succeed in English life.

As I walk around the Parks I see, sitting on a bench, a South African novelist who once gave me a terrible review and I quickly detour. Her accent reaches me with all the harshness of a corncrake as I hurry by. Although I can sometimes hear a South African accent in myself, it has more or less gone, like my father's, but I am super-sensitive to its tones in others. In the old apartheid days it seemed to me a shameful thing, but now I see that what is shameful, or at best petty, is to try to disguise your origins. Waiting to go up to Oxford, I worked in the wine cellar at Harrods. One of my co-workers was a Jamaican, who told me that after six years in England I was the first real Englishman he had met. I didn't disabuse him. That first term in Oxford as I made friends – three or four of whom are still among my closest – I seemed, in a minor Jeffrey Archerish fashion, to have embarked on a re-invention. Archer was floating around Oxford at that time, a mature student who was already the subject of rumour. I remember being invited to a dining club at Brasenose and being told that Jeffrey was not actually a member of the college as he claimed, but somehow had been appointed

Captain of Oxford Athletics anyway. I remember, too, auditioning for a play, *Incitatus*, and feeling humiliated by the fact that I pronounced Leda, the lover of a swan, as 'Layda', and having been corrected by the director, a Wykehamist. The part was given to Richard Heffer, who went on to become a professional actor. Two other actors achieved some success: Diana Quick and Maria Aitken. Later I played Duperret – 'charming, handsome and full of zest' – in the Balliol–Lady Margaret Hall production of *Marat Sade*. The dress rehearsal in Great Coxwell tithe barn near Faringdon was marked by the fact that Marat and I were completely smashed on mead, eccentrically served at the closest pub to the barn, and that Marat fell into the duck pond on the way to the barn and emerged with large patches of green pond life attached, pointillist-style, to his toga, and then Charlotte Corday slapped me in the face when I followed the instruction of the director, which, sober, I had previously failed to put into effect, to molest her vigorously. Oddly enough, although I can't remember the actress's name or her face, I can remember her small orange-shaped breasts. In the general madness nobody noticed either the verdant Marat in his bath or Charlotte giving me an unscripted smack in the face. 'Dearest Charlotte, you must return to your friends the pious nuns.' – *Whack*.

The Parks – there were once two, long united, which explains the plural – is another lovely place. When I come up from London it is not the unique redwoods from Szechwan – once believed extinct – nor the perfect cricket pavilion, nor the glimpses of the river beyond that strike me, but the surprise of clean, ordered, public spaces. It takes me some time to remember that this is how public spaces are meant to be. Oxford has its share of ugly corners and sink estates and heroin addicts with manky dogs, but the first impression I have as I enter the plain and cross Magdalen Bridge is a sense of relief: it's still there. In Islington, despite its reputation as the home of the forward-thinking, there is a very discernible air of aggression. The streets, heroically cleaned by Polish immigrants, are filthy again within hours. I spend some time, unfruitfully, pondering the question of why the local children find it so onerous to walk two paces to the nearest bin, and why local youths are able to steal and race scooters around without fear; but even as I do so I see that I am becoming ridiculous. Meanwhile the middle classes pursue their own agenda, quite different from those who live around them. From the early hours I see young mothers who drive scores of miles a week transporting their children to and from private schools, to music or maths, to swimming, or to elaborate birthday parties. I see them, faces drawn but determined, fighting the traffic, harassed by traffic wardens, children strapped in the back as if this restraint is a necessary condition of getting into a good university – Oxford and Cambridge if possible, Edinburgh or Bristol if not – their little tired pale faces wafting by the urban shambles.

Of course, I know that those who live in Oxford have their particular day-to-day problems, but the fact of living close to some of the most beautiful buildings and landscapes in Britain is surely some compensation. This tricky sense I have of the beauty of Oxford is inseparable from the fact that the centre of Oxford is still whole, a complete, if small, universe. For a few years that is just what it becomes: reading a biography of Peter Cook recently, I was struck by his remark that when he finished at Cambridge he was qualified only to spend his life in Cambridge. Radcliffe Square, which Berlin so loved, seems to me to be the heart of Oxford. His first rooms at All Souls look across the Hawksmoor-designed North Quad to the Radcliffe Camera and the spire of St Mary's. The North Quad is certainly one of the most beautiful in Oxford – 'masterly', says Casson – with the Codrington Library on the north side, Hawksmoor's towers to the east and the cloisters to the west. The gates are decorated with the All Souls mallard. The feeling I always have is that Radcliffe Square is the heart of this little sovereign state, and that All Souls, framing one side of the square, is its intellectual power plant. I had only once been to All Souls until I recently went on a tour of the college. Strangely I knew one current prize fellow and there he was, sole occupant of the magnificent Codrington Library.

The library is absolutely vast, at least a hundred and fifty feet long, one of the grandest I have ever seen, the floor in black-and-white slabs of marble, the two-tiered bookshelves painted a grey-green colour. Urns and large statues of Sir Christopher Codrington, benefactor, and Sir William Blackstone, the great jurist and fellow of the college who was closely involved with the library for many years, adorn the entrance. Anyway, here was young Tom in solitary tranquillity, working away on his doctorate. Actually the marmoreal calm of All Souls is not quite what it seems. Since 1867 the library has been open to suitably serious people and to 'duly recommended' undergraduate or graduate students, but only fellows may browse the shelves unsupervised. Prize fellows are elected for seven years after rigorous exams. It was not always so. For nearly two hundred years many of the founders' kin were able to claim fellowships without having to do anything at all. With the convulsions of the mid-nineteenth century, All Souls had to change. A first-class degree is the minimum requirement for candidature, rather than a blood relationship to the founder.

The Common Room, where fellows can eat and take coffee, at the back of the Hawksmoor towers, opens on to a small garden with a new and, of course, controversial fountain. Any suggestion that it might have come in a box from B&Q is scotched by the inscription on the stone, which is in Latin. Young Tom showed me his rooms looking down on to the North Quad. This is the fantasy of Oxford life, a view across one of the most beautiful spaces in Oxford to Christopher Wren's great sundial.

Tom told me that in his first or second year he

had taken part in the legendary Mallard Supper. The mallard is the heraldic symbol of All Souls. In the first year of every century, the mallard, seen in a dream in the fifteenth century by the founder, Archbishop Chichele, whose name is given to All Souls-sponsored professors, is celebrated in a ceremony of extraordinary silliness. The fellows march around with staves and torches, whooping and yelling for the bird. Some fellows – presumably the younger ones – even appear on the roof. Lord Mallard, carried in a chair, leads the Mallard Circumambulation and at the end of the procession he produces a stick with a dead duck spiked on the end of it. He then sings the Mallard Song so that it rings out over Oxford. In 1901 Lord Mallard was Cosmo Gordon Lang, a future Archbishop of Canterbury, who was to be involved in the abdication controversy. In 2001 the Lord Mallard was Martin West, Senior Research Fellow, and he was carried at the front of the procession in the same chair that had been used in 1901. For the first time there were women fellows taking part.

In fact the Mallard Song is sung twice every year, at the November Gaudy and at the Bursar's Dinner in March. Tom finds it poignant that, while he should have been there, Berlin missed it by four years, after being a fellow for sixty years. I wondered if the quiet perfection of the place could be oppressive to a young man or woman, a sentence rather than a liberation. There is something about All Souls, with its great wealth and its absence of students, that suggests what a lot of people find maddening about Oxford. After a damning Franks Report, All Souls managed to avoid the horror of taking students by setting up generous funding for visiting fellows, and continued to help Harris Manchester College financially. The most famous modern Warden of All Souls, John Sparrow, was bored by academic life. He was too lazy, a don told me, to devise a plan when the pressure was applied to the college to modernise, particularly to take students. Sparrow, for all his raffish, if louche, reputation, spent his last years in miserable retirement on the outskirts of Oxford near the Iffley Road, often drunk. Typical of his meagre output was this little, late, verse:

I'm accustomed to my deafness
To my dentures I'm resigned
I can cope with my bifocals
But – oh dear – I miss my mind.

It's difficult for the outsider not to find something perverse about this very real aspect of Oxford unless he regards Oxford's playful manner as ironic or picturesque. Berlin was very conscious of the opprobrium that Oxford was attracting forty years ago. He wrote to his friend Raimund von Hofmannsthal:

> It is impossible to convey in America the full degree of prejudice against Oxford and Cambridge in the present Labour Government – equality is a noble ideal, and in its interests Oxford and Cambridge require reform – but when the desire for social justice takes resentful and emotional forms, it leads to repression and gratuitous damage rather than reform.

As I have mentioned prejudice against Oxford, it is time for me to come clean. At Oxford I played polo, and was part of the team that beat Cambridge 11–1. It's never seemed to me – I haven't played polo since – something to advertise, because the very fact of polo gave ammunition to those who thought Oxford was the preserve of toffs with too much money. It also made me faintly uneasy, as a penniless South African with – self-proclaimed – intellectual interests, to be rushing about on polo ponies.

Still here it is, an *apologia pro vita mea*: at my college there was an Australian called Chris Ashton. He came from a distinguished polo-playing family, and he knew that I could ride. As a boy in Johannesburg during holidays from boarding school in Cape Town, I used to hang around some riding stables owned by a Polish cavalry major, where I had learned to ride and I had taken part enthusiastically in gymkhanas and hunter trials. (Johannesburg had a drag hunt with a pack of foxhounds, the scent dragged by an African in full kit, riding an immaculate hunter. I find it hard to believe now, looking back down the years.)

Anyway, Ashton had read a notice saying that the Oxford Polo Club needed new members, and was offering a camp over the Easter vacation for those who wanted to learn. We signed up, and reported at Woolmer's Park in Hertfordshire, the home of the Lucas family. Claire Lucas and her boyfriend Simon Tomlinson – now her husband – were undergraduates second and polo fanatics first. Simon had been in the Inniskilling Dragoon Guards and came to Oxford on an Army Scholarship. Claire was studying agriculture. She went on to be the best woman polo player in the world. Woolmer's Park was a huge Georgian house with two polo fields. Everywhere you looked you could see the alert, rather pragmatic, heads of polo ponies peering over stable doors or going through their paces somewhere on the broad acres around the house.

Claire, her father and one or two imported specialists taught us the rudiments of polo. Even without owning a string of ponies or any equipment, polo was expensive. I had saved some money from my tour-guiding of the previous summer and I bought myself some polo boots for £10 from a small ad in *Horse and Hound*. That vacation passed in sheer joy. We were well fed and spent our days galloping about trying not to maim the ponies. It never really occurred to me to enquire about the finances of all this, or to worry about the possibility that I was heading for ruination. For the next three summers I played polo for Oxford, although I had little money: my breeches in the photograph my mother so proudly kept on display for visitors – to demonstrate that I had joined the aristocracy – are very visibly torn. Simon one day said to me that I really had to have my own pony.

The polo club had about five ponies, kept in primitive conditions near Kirtlington, and Simon and Claire had, I think, two or three. Anyway Simon decided I should borrow the money and he would be my security. We walked into the National Westminster Bank in the High and made our request for a loan to the manager. Simon had a small portfolio of shares his father had left him, and he offered them as security for the £350. When I saw the revival of *Donkey's Years* I was reminded of the bank manager. He was like the student nobody remembers at a Gaudy, who always wanted to mix with the roaring boys and have his own colourful waistcoat from one of the dining societies. He seemed to be thrilled to lend me the money. He had, he said, never had a request like it. I think he meant he had never met real old-fashioned toffs before. Of course I thought, in my treacherous way, how ridiculous it was.

A few months later, when I collected my pony on the dockside at Southampton, among a large shipment the Lucas family had acquired in Argentina one pony, who never quite became sane, refused to walk forwards and nearly backed right off the dock and into the water below. Mimosa, my pony, had a curiously shaped head, apparently the result of an accident out on the pampas, but she proved to be astonishingly willing. I loved that pony, although the affection was not returned; whenever she saw me booted and spurred, she would try to move away, although when informally ridden, bareback in nothing but a head-collar, we got on well. We beat Cambridge three times and won the Whitbread Cup, the prize for lower goal polo, twice. Not long ago, for the first time in some years, I spoke to Claire Tomlinson on the phone and I mentioned that I had seen that her son Luke was one of those who invaded the House of Commons in the fox-hunting cause. 'Yes,' she said, 'cool, wasn't it?' I wondered if 'cool' was the right word, but the protean aspect of my nature accommodated quickly to what she meant. It was nothing to do with democracy or vandalism or hooliganism; it was an upper-class sort of stunt, designed to demonstrate something to the wretched polytechnic lecturers in the House of Commons: it was cool.

6

John Plamenatz, my supervisor, was elected a Prize Fellow of All Souls at about the same time that Berlin was elected, in 1932. When he agreed to be my supervisor he was based at Nuffield College, endowed by Lord Nuffield, who had started making his cars in Longwall Street at his bicycle-repair works. From there he spread out into the green fields of Cowley, where he created an enormous factory to produce the Morris Oxford and Morris Minor. Betjeman, characteristically, believed that Nuffield had destroyed Oxford. He also had a nostalgia for an earlier, imagined, England, which he found in suburban North Oxford:

> Where once there grazed the cows
> Emancipated children swing on apple boughs.

In truth it's hard to imagine exactly what sort of England John Betjeman would have liked: there would have been no industry, no conifers in gardens, no businessmen, no cars, no litter and no common people. In a way it was an England that would have corresponded more to Tolkien's Middle Earth than anything recognisable. In fact Betjeman was far from predictable: he was an early member and supporter of the Establishment Club, which did so much to change British attitudes to authority. All his life he was caught in a productive tension between his sensitivity to his lower-middle-class origins and his friendships with the artistic and well-born, something which, in a fashion, I also experienced at Oxford, although colonials were exempt from the lingering effects of class judgement. Still, I remember people in Trinity talking of 'grammar-school gnomes' or 'grey men'. Now, the decline of the grammar school has been mythologised by these same people as a typically Bolshevik manoeuvre.

One day I was walking down to Nuffield College to seek out Plamenatz's rooms, where we would discuss Marshal Tito, who, Plamenatz said, had much in common with the subject of my thesis, Oliver Cromwell. I was exercising my rights as a reader to pass through the Bodleian, and I saw that there was an exhibition of Betjeman memorabilia, which included his teddy bear, Archie, and his elephant, Jumbo. They are both extraordinarily worn from fervent affection. Betjeman's poem about Archie is a textbook case of the only child who requires a friend:

> And if an analyst one day
> Of school of Adler, Jung or Freud
> Should take this agéd bear away,
> Then, oh my God, the dreadful void!
> Its draughty darkness could but be
> Eternity, Eternity.

It was Archie that inspired Evelyn Waugh's Algernon in *Brideshead Revisited*. The exhibition was full of insights for anyone interested in the whole nexus, which is still in some minds the defining myth of Oxford: Waugh uses Betjeman's bear for the greatest Oxford novel ever written; an exhibition shows that the manuscript of Betjeman's *Summoned by Bells* is heavily edited by John Sparrow, the Warden of All Souls, who has a homosexual relationship with Maurice Bowra, the Warden of Wadham, author of scabrous poetry, whose subject is sometimes the imagined sex life of the newly married Penelope and John Betjeman, with interventions by her horse. Bowra himself, whose prose – to quote Sparrow – 'was unreadable and his verse unprintable', is famous for his wit and his energising qualities. He gathers round him an extraordinary circle. He and Berlin are good friends, but Bowra's allure begins to fade just about at the point where Berlin becomes a world figure. The Oxford circle is cruelly squared. There is a rather poignant letter from Berlin saying how pleased Bowra is with his knighthood:

> The principal item of home news is the knighthood of the Warden of Wadham. Although on the whole affably dealt with, except by the *Manchester Guardian* which wondered a little why it should have occurred, and the *Observer* which printed the most offensive and vicious attack I have ever seen delivered on a human being by a British newspaper, accusing my jolly old friend of corrupting the youth by teaching them that malice was courage and gossip was art. It led off with the headline 'Clever fellow knighted', gave an offensive description of Dr Bowra's appearance and

> character, said that he was a mixture of eighteenth-century man of letters and a 'bullyboy', whatever that may be. Said that on his first visit to the United States he was a great social success, stressing 'first' and 'social': that his books were stodgy and pedagogic and finally that he was at his worst in dealing with serious matters such as his attitude to anti-Nazi Germans engaged in opposing Hitler.

This last is a reference to Adam von Trott.

Although Betjeman famously claimed that he was 'failed in divvers', the curator of this exhibition discovered that Betjeman did eventually pass in divinity. But Betjeman never forgave Lewis. He even refused to meet Lewis in later years. His *Chronicles of Narnia* achieved a worldwide popular success surprising for a highly intellectual man. In *The Corrections* by Jonathan Franzen, *Narnia* is read by one of the family almost desperately, as a kind of moral text for his uninterested children. Oxford dons' novels, it seems, have largely been successful only when they have contained something childlike. And you cannot avoid the conclusion that there is often something childlike about Oxford dons. International success for

Lewis was to be replicated by his friend J.R.R. Tolkien. The most popular part of any Oxford literary tour is the section devoted to these two, the mainstay of the Inklings, a literary group gathered around Tolkien, Lewis, David Cecil, Nevill Coghill and others, most of whom believed in the virtues of narrative. To this day groups of aficionados can be found in the Eagle and Child, where the Inklings met on Tuesday mornings.

When I arrived at Oxford, the Bowra era had long since passed, even though Bowra was physically still there, but he was suffering the effects of growing old in Oxford, something that can be more pronounced than elsewhere. When Elizabeth Bowen returned after the war to live in Oxford, where she had been a social success between 1923 and 1924, she discovered that, while the scenery had not been moved, the actors had gone, something that Auden also discovered during his final stay in Oxford. Because Oxford is a city devoted to youth, it deals out these intimations of mortality ruthlessly. But I see now that the most important aspect of this brief and conflicted period in Oxford's history is that it has come to represent a persistent image of Oxford: the hearties who chase Paul Pennyfeather from his room in *Decline and Fall*, the aesthetes like Harold Acton, Betjeman and his teddy bears and the arch social circle around Bowra, all these have coloured the public perception. But this myth obscures the enormous achievements of the time: in Philosophy J.L. Austin, A.J. Ayer and Berlin were giants, although Berlin gave up philosophy for the history of ideas. Graham Greene, Anthony Powell and Henry Green were all more or less contemporaries of Waugh, as were W.H. Auden and Louis MacNeice.

MacNeice wrote:

That having once been to the University of Oxford
You can never really again
Believe anything that anyone says and that of
course is an asset
In a world like ours.

There were also important advances in medicine and the sciences, and soon Oxford historians, including Hugh Trevor-Roper, A.J.P. Taylor, J.H. Plumb, Christopher Hill, Alan Bullock and Eric Hobsbawm, were creating a hegemony all of their own. Trevor-Roper's wonderful letters to Bernard Berenson have gone some way to restoring his reputation after his 1983 blunder in hastily authenticating the Hitler diaries for the *Sunday Times*, of which he was a non-executive director. I find it hard to believe now that while I was meandering around Oxford, Berlin, Maurice Bowra and A.L.Rowse – who was once in love with Adam von Trott and proclaimed that he could spend the rest of his life with him – were alive and well. There was controversy before the war about the idea that some of the leading lights at All Souls were appeasers, Geoffrey Dawson, Editor of *The Times*, and Warden Sparrow among them. Berlin, from the date of Adam von Trott's ill-advised letter to the *Manchester Guardian* in 1934, was vehemently opposed to any appeasement. At the same time there was a frivolous election for the parliamentary seat of Oxford, with Quintin Hogg standing on an appeasement platform. Von Trott's pleas that the new National Socialist regime be understood for what it was, a natural reaction to German humiliation that would fade away with Hitler's success, resulted in 1939 in the famous confrontation with Bowra, who asked von Trott to leave his rooms immediately. Bowra had asked von Trott what he thought the British should do about

Hitler, and von Trott suggested they should grant Hitler the German-speaking lands he had taken, because that would be the end of his appeal for the German people.

To me the most interesting aspect of von Trott's attempts to keep his Oxford friends on side, to ask them to give some credit and some understanding to what was a very real and widespread German opposition to Hitler, is that he believed that Oxford had enormous influence in Whitehall. To some extent it was true. The Vice Chancellor of the university, his old Balliol chum A.D. Lindsay, arranged meetings for von Trott at the highest level. After my novel, *The Song Before It Is Sung*, was published in 2007, I discovered that the ties that bound von Trott and his friends in England, including some members of the Astor family, were still very strong. They attacked me for distorting the facts of von Trott's life, heedless of the fact that this was a novel.

The truth is that von Trott, as Berlin was fond of reminding him, invariably fell back on Hegel when backed into a philosophical corner. And this fatally undermined his credibility as a spokesman for another Germany, the secret Germany of the poet Stefan George, a Germany with a mystical and manifest destiny in the world. Berlin was far more inclined to Turgenev's pragmatic liberalism. As he demonstrated triumphantly in the fifties, he had come to the conclusion that human values can often be in conflict and that the aim of any government should be to ensure basic freedoms from certain restrictions, rather than to postulate some future Utopia that could be reached only through Fascism or Marxism or religion.

As I walk down towards Nuffield to see John Plamenatz's rooms, I am ashamed of myself. Although I knew that John Plamenatz had come from Montenegro, I had, with all the insouciance of youth, demonstrated no curiosity about his history, and I had no idea of the background to his and Berlin's interests in the nature of government. He once welcomed Berlin's company saying that whenever he was in a room with Englishmen he felt alone. Nor had I heard of Adam von Trott, although it was only twenty-one years since he was brutally executed. I understood, of course, from my South African upbringing that ideologies can have very real and very dangerous consequences. When I knew him Plamenatz was a fellow of Nuffield, although he was soon to go back to All Souls as Chichele Professor of Social and Political Thought. Chichele professorships are as prestigious as it gets in Oxford. Plamenatz was sent as a boy from Montenegro to a public school in Britain. His family in Montenegro was very distinguished: his father was the kingdom's last prime minister. Despite this background he was fond of making remarks like, 'As a simple peasant I can't answer this question,' or, 'We mountain people always fight for our rights.' I now discover that Plamenatz has recently been taken up in his home country, where he was little known. I have applied to join the newly formed Plamenatz Society, although for some Balkan reason I have had no reply. Perhaps Nuffield from its infinite resources can support the resurgence of interest in this great man. All I really remembered of him personally was the wonderfully kind and sensitive notes he gave me after my thesis, which was entitled *The Political Thought of Oliver Cromwell, with particular reference to the concept of the honest party*, had been rejected at my first viva with a request to add some detail and a fuller bibliography. I have kept his notes:

> 6 p.m.
> July 27, 1969
> Dear Mr Cartwright,
> I have now had our additional chapter. I like it, though I wonder whether it is long enough or detailed enough to fill the gap that your examiners thought needed filling. I think I had better ask Mr Thomas about that.

He goes on to give some detailed criticism, very gently couched, and ends this way:

> I hope these comments are of some use. I do think the chapter needs to be longer (considerably longer) to make your points adequately.
> With best wishes,
> Yours,
> John Plamenatz

I regret deeply that I was so little interested in the rich life of John Plamenatz. I think that when we are young we don't naturally have a curiosity about people who appear to be much older and the reason for that is that we are not yet concerned to make sense of our own position in the universe by comparison with others. I have Plamenatz's letter in front of me as I write this, and I find myself touching it, as if it can yield something of my far from admirable youth.

After the first disastrous viva, with Keith Thomas peering at me sceptically through thick glasses, which reduced me to a state of near imbecility, I was awarded my BLitt by the examiners, who included Maurice Ashley, at the second attempt. Ashley urged me to join the Cromwell Society. I couldn't tell him that at that moment I wanted to forget Cromwell for ever. But I haven't forgotten Cromwell. Indeed there seem to be more and more aspects of Cromwell I recognise in the world. Essentially Cromwell was a fundamentalist of a very contemporary kind. His absolute conviction that he had God's ear allowed him to forget that he had undertaken the revolution of 1642 in the name of the ordinary people.

The oddest thing about Nuffield is the immense, eleven-storey tower, which is from an earlier, more brutal, plan for the college. The architects who designed it were not sufficiently interested in Lord Nuffield's own hints that he wanted something vernacular for his money, and the rest of the plan was re-drawn, leaving only the tower from the original. The tower houses one of Oxford's best libraries and is devoted to the social sciences. It straddles the main hall, which has the appearance of a huge beer-hall in Innsbruck or Munich. Plamenatz's rooms, where we had discussed Tito, had been restored so that I did not recognise them, but still I felt that by making the effort I was in some very small way atoned for my negligence.

A city is of course a place, an accumulation of bricks, glass, architecture and landscape. But more than that, it is the sense that these material objects contain its accumulated history. A few cities have a deep personal significance for individuals, but none, I would guess, carries a heavier load of significance for hundreds of thousands than Oxford. As I leave Nuffield and walk down to the newly restored Castle, with the Said Wafiq Business School rising elegantly out of the surrounding mean streets leading to the station – 'these slums which connect Oxford to the world', as Max Beerbohm described them – I wonder what value this sense of personal significance has. Is it like that emotion you feel at the cinema, a kind of self-centred rehearsal of real emotion, or is it a sense of mortality? In Africa there is a common delusion among white people that Africa, with its magnificent landscapes, is somehow there to complement them. In South Africa today many whites are clutching at straws, so that the weather, the landscape, the vistas are prized, as if they were expressly designed to give some meaning to their lives. Oxford, I see, speaks to me wistfully and falsely of my youth, and I wonder if my love of the place isn't really just as self-serving, perhaps nothing more than Nicolson's marmalade effect, a nostalgic frisson, an emotion that is gratifying but delusional. Incidentally, when Alice tumbles down the rabbit hole she passes a jar of marmalade, which turns out to be empty.

You can climb the remains of the Norman tower, built in 1071, for an astonishing view of Oxford. From here the royalists kept a look out for Cromwell's armies when, after the battle of Edgehill in 1642, they made Oxford their capital; for four years the King set up his court in Christ Church. His queen was given Merton, and the flamboyant Prince Rupert lived at St John's; gunpowder was stored in the cloisters of New College. The city was fortified, and you can still see the remains of earthworks in the Warden's Garden at Wadham College and in the garden of Rhodes House. Three battles were fought within a few miles of Oxford. The King put the heat on the university to produce the funds for the war, and a lot of college silver was lost. Corpus Christi hid its silver in beehives and to this day the college is obliged to keep bees in memory of their ruse. A recent exhibition of college silver at the Ashmolean revealed that very little pre-Civil War silver survives, but also demonstrated that the colleges had made good their collections as soon as they could. Richard Foxe, the founder of Corpus in 1517, left the college a salt cellar, the finest example in Oxford of Tudor goldsmithing, and this had pride of place in the exhibition; I wondered how much time it passed in the Corpus beehives. Salt cellars, because of their relative novelty, were highly prized and intricately worked and had a prominent place on Oxford high tables.

In May 1645, Charles sallied forth for the decisive battle of the Civil War, which was lost at Naseby. Early the following year, Cromwell and Fairfax set up camp in Headington, and soon Charles fled the city disguised as a servant. The war was over on 20 June, and the Royalist army left under safe conduct four days later. Charles's reign in Oxford had an extraordinary effect: teaching ceased altogether in favour of endless revels and pageants. When he took possession of the city, Thomas Fairfax put a guard on the Bodleian to ensure that there would be no looting – as the guides are fond of saying – a generous act from a Cambridge man. Legend relates that the Bodleian had refused to lend the King a book, and to this day it never has lent a book.

Now that it has been restored, the Castle is a pleasant precinct, distanced by an ocean of caffè latte from its history, with a boutique hotel fashioned from the old prison, where you can sleep in a converted cell; round about, there are various chain restaurants and cafés. These days Oxford is well off for restaurants; when I arrived, George's in the covered market was just about the only thing resembling a popular café. I have no nostalgia for the old, rather dowdy England that I knew then. Now even the market is chic, and photographed by tourists. We sometimes went to Dudley's for dinner, and the eponymous Dudley, his paunch perched like a Victorian rustic's on a leather belt, would appear at table to insult us in his cheerful, drunken fashion. Half the plates in the restaurant had been stolen from some hotel or pub. Dudley, I was told, gave it all up as he couldn't bear to see another undergraduate. Another time I remember driving back from the George in Dorchester after a dining-club dinner, and hurling plates out of the window at passing cars. These days this sort of behaviour would lead to a well-deserved ASBO; then it was thought – by us anyway – as a commendably light-hearted jape.

I ponder the fact that I could have established a far more fruitful – for me – relationship with John Plamenatz. Perhaps if I had, I might have spent my days in Oxford. It is a common enough fantasy that the academic life would have been quaintly satisfying. But my experience of Oxford dons is that many of them want to break out, at least into print or on radio if not by physical separation. It is as if they see the outside world as more real and more vibrant, where those of us in the so-called real world long for the imagined quietude of Oxford.

I walk up to the covered market and order a cappuccino. I am spending a lot of time trying in some non-specific way to capture the essence of Oxford, as if by hanging around aimlessly I can understand it better. Undergraduates in examination subfusc – white tie, dark suit, gown – are sitting at cafés, some reading feverishly, others relaxing after an exam. In Oxford you can read a book anywhere you like, without attracting attention. I sit and read *Fathers and Sons* by Turgenev, because Isaiah Berlin loved it. It was the subject of his Romanes Lecture of 1970. Berlin said of Turgenev:

> He was concerned, above all, to enter into, to understand, views, ideals, temperaments, both those which he found sympathetic and those by which he was puzzled or repelled . . . Nature, personal relationships, quality of feeling – these are what he understood best, these, and their expression in art. He loved every manifestation of art and beauty as deeply as anyone has ever done. The conscious use of art for ends extraneous to itself, ideological, didactic or utilitarian, and especially as a deliberate weapon in the class war as demanded by the radicals of the 1860s, was detestable to him.

If I had anything so grand as a credo, or even a coherently organised set of beliefs, Berlin's words would largely do. And in my way, in my progress to this unforeseen age, I have often thought of Berlin and Oxford as one. It is

Berlin's humanity which is so appealing: Arthur Schlesinger, historian and friend of JFK, described him as 'this man of surpassing brilliance and singular sweetness'. Almost everyone who knew him – and I have met many – says something similar. Although apparently writing about Turgenev and his urgent desire 'to enter into nature, personal relationships, quality of feeling', Berlin was unmistakably writing about himself (except for a desire to enter into nature).

In the market I enter into a discussion about coffee at Cardew's and I am almost surprised by the kindness of the manager; in London a kind of barely contained brusqueness is the prevailing mode. I have three coffee machines at home, and coffee has taken on the qualities of a fetish for me, something similar to the fetishes on display in the Pitt-Rivers (of the animist rather than the sexual type).

That evening I attend the annual Isaiah Berlin Lecture at Wolfson College. Professor Michael Walzer from Princeton is the speaker. He makes some interesting points about the nature of pioneering political movements, including Indian's Congress Party, Israel's Mapai, and Algeria's FLN. He sees similarities in their histories: in all three the broadly democratic and socialist intentions of the founding fathers are hijacked by fundamentalists and sectarians. In the question and answer session, Muslim students dominate with pointed questions about Israel's behaviour; they are apparently – depressingly – unaware of the nature of a liberal academic lecture, which is to discuss ideas rather than to champion causes. I fervently want to thrust Berlin's lecture on *Fathers and Sons* into their hands and force them to read it.

Oddly enough, *Fathers and Sons* was published no more than a year after the famous Wilberforce–Huxley confrontation, which was essentially about what it means to be human. I see, too, as I head back to London in the night, that a life in Oxford chasing down connections might have driven me crazy. For example, as I drive on into the dark, I remember that Oliver Cromwell, who treated the Irish so harshly, believed quite literally that the Jews were the chosen people and so granted them a new freedom; and I remember that Isaiah Berlin was both a Zionist and an unbeliever, and that his friend Adam von Trott was a hero and a German nationalist. Experience, Henry James said, is an immense spider's web catching every airborne particle blown in the wind.

7

I have admired Valentine Cunningham since his 1997 attack, published in *Prospect*, on Arundhati Roy's novel *The God of Small Things*, which seemed to demonstrate just how wrong the Booker judges can go at times. Cunningham is one of those dons who is as much at home in a radio studio as at a public discussion and rather endearingly up to date, with terms like 'dodgy' and 'bovver boys' littering his criticism. He is a teaching fellow of Corpus Christi College and Professor of English Language and Literature, a personal chair. I had to ask what a personal chair is: it seems that since the nineties Oxford has followed a trend of awarding the title of Professor to individuals of distinction. Essentially this means that they are not holders of one of the traditional endowed chairs, like the Regius and Chichele or the Merton. Merton Professors of English have included J.R.R. Tolkien, Nevill Coghill and John Carey. There is also a Wharton chair of English: nothing is straightforward at Oxford. One academic suggested to me that personal chairs were a means to avoid a brain drain: virtually everybody at a North American university is a professor of one sort or another.

As I was shown to Cunningham's rooms in Corpus I felt again the powerful attraction of Oxford academic life. Corpus is a small college, founded in 1517 (although the dates of foundation seem to be more a question of prestige, like ancient peerages, than of any real importance). It has rather eccentric planting, tomatoes and bamboos and runner beans around the quads, giving it a slightly unkempt look, as though the jungle might close in at any moment.

But the college itself is undeniably beautiful, with a domestic quality that is very appealing. As in the best murder-mystery fiction, it was in this peaceful setting that a bizarre series of incidents resulted, after a decade of strife, in the suicide of Trevor Aston, a fellow of the college, in 1986. Not only had he been a fellow of the college since 1952, but also the college librarian, the university's archivist and one of the editors of its newest history. But he rarely, if ever, published any original work of his own, something of a crime in Oxford. At the same time he had become increasingly prone to drunken and irrational behaviour, which included violent arguments and endless confrontations at college meetings. He appeared to think that he was the keeper of the college's soul, and the final arbiter of its taste, decorating a house he was allowed to use lavishly, consulting the makers of recherché wallpapers and finishes at the college's expense. The President of the College, Sir Kenneth Dover, the distinguished classicist, admitted in his memoirs that he had fantasised about causing Aston's death by an act of omission, such as not reporting a suicide call. He had even discussed consulting lawyers to see if he could in some way be regarded as culpable if Aston killed himself. 'But it was clear to me by now that Trevor and the college must somehow be separated. My problem was one which I feel compelled to define with brutal candour: how to kill him without getting into trouble.'

In the event, after being told by Dover that his re-election as a fellow had been passed only by the narrowest of margins, Aston did kill himself. Dover reported that:

The next day I got up from a long, sound sleep and looked out of the window across the fellows' garden. I cannot say for sure that the sun was shining, but I certainly felt it was. I said to myself, slowly, 'Day One of Year One of the Post-Astonian Era'. For a little while, I even regretted my decision to retire the following year.

It is not news that Oxford can be a nest of vipers and that the enclosed, rather inward-looking spaces foster ideas of intrigue and murder. Corpus seemed like the ideal place to discuss the Oxford don's alleged love of the detective novel. Cunningham's rooms are spectacular, with a view out over gardens and on to Christ Church. No prospect in Oxford is more enticing, because the openness, almost a prairie, that greets you is such a surprise after making your way through various quads and portals.

The main room is high, with books reaching to the ceiling. It's a strange fetish, the book fetish. It's as if being in the presence of books delivers exactly what a fetish object promises, supernatural powers, or power over others. Certainly, in my recent excursions to Oxford, I have felt that entering a great canyon of books like this one puts you at a disadvantage: after all you have to assume that your host has read all the books, as you gaze nervously around. I see the young undergraduate coming for his first tutorial. If he or she had imagined that in the Internet age it would not be strictly necessary to read too many books, this sight of a don's study would come as a shock. The undergraduate may have imagined that a quick trawl through literary theory would have been enough. Cunningham has himself written very well about the deleterious effect of literary theory: he says that reading has sometimes been seen as secondary to theory in English departments. For those of us who write but are not academics, literary theory seems rather remote, a kind of acrostic itself, an intellectual exercise that doesn't necessarily require any deep sense of language or style or life. It bears the same relationship to literature that trainspotting does to travel; you are required only to stand at the station, and never required to travel.

Cunningham is highly entertaining. I ask him about the influence of the twenties and thirties generation, the *Brideshead* generation, on Oxford and the wider perception of Oxford. Cunningham explains to me that there were certain people at Oxford – he cites Lord David Cecil and Nevill Coghill – who kept alive this tradition well into the post-war years. Coghill, he says, was slack, 'crap at Shakespeare'. And Cecil had formally decreed that nothing good had been written since 1914 and that no modern literature should therefore be studied. Tolkien, progenitor of the Hobbit, and C.S. Lewis actually wanted the Victorians removed from the syllabus as too modern; philology should be the single most important field of study. But by the end of the war there were other pressures; grammar-school boys, like John Carey, and ex-servicemen had come to Oxford and they were not interested in or enthralled by the *Brideshead* world. It still had its devotees: Cunningham says that when Helen Gardner came to Oxford from an unimpeachably ordinary, leftish background, she was entranced by the Cecil claque and their reactionary views. Cecil, in Cunningham's account, was a parody of a parody, proclaiming that 'we are all working class now' in his squeaky, etiolated voice. John Bayley, Old Etonian and army officer, who was almost shot by the IRA, was made of steely material, but Oxford turned him frivolous, Cunningham claims. Bayley was attracted to Iris Murdoch, whose philosophy may have been intensely serious, but whose fiction, according to Cunningham, is frivolous and populist, also resting on a kind of *Brideshead* view of the world. Cunningham describes this as the hegemony of the twenties and thirties generations. He tells of going in the sixties as an undergraduate to a class in New College given by Bayley and Cecil and being told that it was for graduates only. Later, as a graduate, he was told the same class was for undergraduates only. He had the distinct sense that it was open only to those Bayley and Cecil found congenial.

Some of this group that gathered around Cecil and Coghill promoted the Authorised Version of the Bible and Anglo-Catholicism along with their dislike of contemporary literature. It seems to have been part of a deliberately reactionary, defiant stance. We discuss the connection between this strongly religious and nostalgic group and homosexuality. I suggest that possibly homosexuals found it congenial to belong to what in a sense was a self-selected group. Although it seems clear that the *Brideshead* effect lived on, both as an image of Oxford and as a reality among faculty members, there is no satisfactory theory to embrace Waugh, Betjeman, Bowra, Sparrow, Tolkien,

Lewis, Cecil, Bayley and many others, although a kind of reactionary and provocative public stance is common to most of them. Curiously, something of this survived in the *Spectator*. I remember Ian Buruma's account of his days there: one day he guessed he might be in the wrong place when the then editor, Charles Moore, asked him which version of the Bible he used. It was the 'used' that struck him as most incongruous. It was, he felt, the almost obligatory subscription to what were thought of as traditional English values, a deliberate and knowing reaction.

Cunningham illuminated the famous taste for detective fiction of Oxford dons, which may have contributed to their relative paucity of literary production: it is a kind of relaxation after hard intellectual effort. In the thirties, he said, people associated the huge popularity of crossword puzzles with poetic difficulty, in the Empson and Eliot style. It was easy to make the association for dons, because donnish persons write them and feature in them. In A.N. Wilson's novel *The Healing Art*, the narrator notices the preponderance of detective fiction on a dying don's shelves, with snobbish disgust. A.N. Wilson is himself in speech and appearance almost a parody of the dons of an earlier time, so attesting to the power of the myth.

But I also see, I think, juvenilia and public-school humour linking the generations since the twenties. A more interesting question is whether or not Oxford writers like Waugh and Betjeman were always burdened with the sense that you could be both enamoured of the life and detached from it. It may anyway be one of the characteristics of the Oxford-educated to take nothing too seriously; I think there is a tendency in Oxford to think that the narrowly applied and the practically directed are second-rate or useful only to scientists. It's a form of intellectual snobbery, but it is a hard thing to put the genie back in the bottle. Yet, Cunningham says, while the *Brideshead* myth was being fabricated and perpetuated, there were many other significant things going on in science, which is an infinitely more straightforward measure of achievement. But science is not part of the Oxford myth: the Oxford myth is concerned only with aesthetes, hearties, and aristocrats. After all Jay Gatsby was an Oxford man, and Bill Clinton was derided for the same reason during his sex scandal.

I tell Cunningham that I think Oxford people underestimate the power of the myth. Outside Oxford, Oxford has an independent existence as a brand: it carries far more weight than Cambridge in the world at large. The distinguished journalist R.W. Johnson, for example, told me that the description of himself on his card as a Fellow Emeritus of Magdalen College Oxford, carries immense weight in Africa, which is his area of operation. And you can't imagine Jeffrey Archer passing himself off as a Cambridge graduate, even though he occupies Rupert Brooke's parsonage in Cambridge. In the myth, Cambridge is for the clodhopper (Waugh's word) and the lab-rat, although the comedy and satire revolution of the sixties, seventies and eighties was born there. I also ask Cunningham about the research suggesting that the tutorial system is backed by undergraduates: he agrees that whatever its merits it is seen as having class, something utterly distinctive and part of the cultural capital that comes with having been at Oxford. In fact this cultural capital (a term coined in French sociological circles) is exactly what anxious parents want for their children, as Stephen Spender admitted in his letter about his own son's prospects.

Still, Cunningham is not a great believer in the system. He says that it does not exist as in the myth, a Socratic dialogue between tutor and undergraduate. In fact, he says, it has not really operated in that way since the seventies, the tutor tuning and tweaking the young mind. The tutorial burden and the possibility of having to spend one hour at least with an unresponsive undergraduate has led some tutors to favour classes for two hours at a time in which, as Cunningham puts it, real work can be done. Peer-group pressure is also helpful, the smartest members of the group leading the way. Teaching is more than ever necessary, because many undergraduates arrive without having read much. When they are given a test on two or three of the many books they are supposed to have read after being accepted by Corpus, they are often shocked. I notice that this treatment, administered humanely and without any lives being lost, is often applied to freshers. But the tutorial system is still a living component of the Oxford myth and a real part of the allure of Oxford.

Cunningham takes me on a short tour of the college. In the fellows' garden I see the two beehives where bees have been kept for hundreds of years. You find this kind of tradition, like the striking of the clock in Christ Church's Tom Quad 101 times, and the Mallard Song of All Souls, either silly or picturesque. I waver. I peer through the keyhole into the Dean's Garden of Christ Church, made famous in *Alice*. In typical Oxford fashion the Dean of Christ Church is not some nondescript cleric, but the head of house – as Oxford quaintly puts it – of the most glamorous college in Oxford. So different it is that its clock is set five minutes after GMT, its dons are called students and it is known as 'The House' by its members. In fact Christ Church has been a sort of princely state within Oxford, socially a cut above the other colleges and until relatively recently the destination of the titled and the wealthy undergraduate. It was towards Christ Church that Waugh and Betjeman cast envious glances and it was at Christ Church that Harold Acton read poetry to the flannelled fools passing beneath his window in the direction of the river. Acton's most famous stunt was to recite *The Waste Land* through a megaphone at a party in Worcester. Oddly enough, Waugh denied that Anthony Blanche was modelled on Acton, claiming that he was more closely based on Brian Howard,

Acton's close friend and fellow aesthete from Eton. Christ Church has an art collection many small cities would be proud of, including a Dürer, a van Dyck, a Raphael, Tintoretto's *Martyrdom of St Lawrence* and a collection of Old Master drawings. In Christ Church the college servants still wear bowler hats on high days.

As I leave Corpus Christi and walk through Oriel Square, past the imposing rear gates of Christ Church, I wonder how it is exactly that the *Brideshead* myth has cast such a long shadow. I think about what Cunningham said: the Oxford myth is both attractive and repellent. And, as he pointed out, we wouldn't be discussing it at all if it were not part of us. This myth, I think, stands in the way of a true understanding of Oxford. After many years as a writer and at one time an adviser to the Liberals and the SDP, I know that myths stick and achieve a reality of their own. In 1979 Michael Foot decried the influence of the media image of politicians and urged the public to read the Labour Manifesto as an antidote, blissfully unaware that perception is a form of reality in politics. In my own direct experience, the *Spitting Image* caricature of David Steel as a little manikin sitting in David

Owen's pyjama pocket did him immense damage. The truth was that Steel was the more straightforward and effective politician.

I am conscious, as I walk happily down one of the most evocative streets in Oxford, that I am unable to see the city as a separate entity from the university. The attraction of Oxford is not to do with the town: I feel – already – slightly guilty that I have so little interest in the town, but also I excuse myself with the thought that the town and the university are joined in a kind of chiaroscuro.

But still, as I head towards the Ashmolean, I wonder if I shouldn't be including something more about the city in this book. I could write a few words about Lord Nuffield, William Morris, and his bicycle works in Longwall Street. But then I fall back on the resolution I made at the very beginning: this is essentially my account of Oxford; not a guide to Oxford or a rehashing of well-known anecdotes, but an attempt to explain how as a colonial boy I found this place worked on me, plumping up my rather dried-out world, and how its combination of beauty, contrariness, deep-seated liberalism, scepticism and tradition have provided a muted background to my life. I remember, too, what Colin

Lucas told me, that each generation of Oxford people takes what it requires from Oxford, and refashions it. And that Valentine Cunningham said that it's part of us, even if we dislike it, echoing Larkin. I never dream about the town and in fact it is unlikely I will, because every memory I have of Oxford and every feeling I have for it is unmistakably and for ever applied, like impasto, to my earlier self when I was unaware of the town as a separate entity. Even now, the town seems to be a pale presence, so fierce is the force of the university's radiance, both real and imagined, with its sublime buildings and parks and quads, and the pressing insistence of its uniqueness and humanity.

8

The point about Oxford's gardens and quads and nearby villages is that they enter for ever the lives of many who were at Oxford. As the Indian writer Dom Moraes remembered it from Bombay, 'Those gardens far away explain my lives.' I understand this sentiment perfectly, although why this should be is more complicated. It is no use saying that this is a false consciousness or an unearned privilege, it is simply the fact that Oxford has a magic, which is, of course, associated with the beauty of the place, but also with a particularly charged time in one's life. As I was researching this book, I asked many of the interviewees to name their favourite places. Henry Hardy – Berlin's editor and publisher – cited Binsey and agreed to walk there with me. I read up my Hopkins in preparation for our visit:

Justin Cartwright

Binsey Poplars, felled 1879

My aspens dear, whose airy cages quelled,
Quelled or quenched in leaves the leaping sun,
All felled, felled, are all felled;
Of a fresh and following folded rank
Not spared, not one That dandled a sandalled
Shadow that swam or sank
On meadow and river and wind-wandering
  weed-winding bank.
O if we but knew what we do
When we delve or hew –
Hack and rack the growing green!
Since country is so tender
To touch, her being so slender,
That, like this sleek and seeing ball
But a prick will make no eye at all,
Where we, even where we mean
To mend her we end her,
When we hew or delve:
After-comers cannot guess the beauty been.
Ten or twelve, only ten or twelve
Strokes of havoc unselve
The sweet especial scene,
Rural scene, a rural scene,
Sweet especial rural scene.

Henry and I set out on a very cold day in March for the sweet especial rural scene from the Banbury Road, crossing the Woodstock Road and entering Little Clarendon Street. These two arteries of North Oxford I used to think of as the kind of veins one found in the overcooked liver at my boarding school in Cape Town. I was fond of gothic metaphor; the surrounding streets no doubt corresponded to the grey and unappealing offal.

Every stone is familiar to Henry. He is bred and conditioned by these streets. Binsey, I feel, is on the outer reaches of his emotional universe, which is contained within the ring road. At the same time, he protests, he has a place in his heart for Lesotho, where he taught. As we cross Walton Street, increasingly chic but still recognisably the habitat of Jude Fawley, I notice that the scruffy margins of the river and the little parcels of untended land, the railway leftovers, are all being built on. Oxford has become a very desirable place for the successful to live, close enough to London, but with all the advantages of space and good schools and beautiful surroundings. Property prices, Henry tells me, are astronomical. So apartment blocks and neo-Edwardian complexes are being shoehorned into unlikely corners. I could embark here on a lament about the way Oxford is changing, but the truth is it is changing a lot less than other places in the world, and every change in Oxford has always been lamented. Hopkins lamented, Betjeman lamented, John Wain lamented. Anyway, all the land as we cross the bridge on to Port Meadow and as far as the eye can see is common land, and beyond that, where we are stepping westward, the fields and cottages are all owned by Christ Church.

Today Port Meadow is flooded and geese and other wild fowl are enjoying their freedom to camp on the islands or paddle aimlessly about. Geese, I think, spend a lot of their lives in a temper. It is only when they fly that they are transubstantiated into something carefree and spiritual. Binsey, which waits for us, has spiritual qualities. Henry points to an old farm barely visible beyond the river, leased by the same family for years, and to the boatyard run by another family. Everything here has a wonderfully familiar, slightly scruffy feel, as though market forces have not yet arrived to tidy the place up. And this, I find, is an obsession with a certain kind of English person, well represented in Oxford, that gentrification and tidying up and too much gleaming paint are in some way pointers to a coarsening of the national spirit, the embrace of materialism. I remember much the same attitude directed towards central heating when I first arrived in England.

We pass the thatched Perch, one of two fishy pubs in the area, the other being the Trout, and now we can see Binsey church in the distance. Henry suddenly exclaims that the horse chestnut trees, which once provided a long avenue to the church and Church Farmhouse, where the Pricketts lived for many years, have gone. Then he recalls that they suffered some sort of disease akin to Dutch elm disease. As we get closer we see that the huge trees have been replaced with limes. Christ Church decided that these will give an 'avenue effect' very quickly, but some people say they are best suited to a supermarket car park. Nothing in Oxford can pass without comment. Incidentally, poplars have a life of only one hundred and fifty years, so it seems Hopkins's lament was misplaced. The poplars that lined the river had to be felled – all felled – because they were exhausted.

For a decade from 1969, Henry used to lodge at the vicarage in Osney; he paid £2.50 per week in rent to the eccentric vicar, Arnold Mallinson, who was fond of young men and played the organ at St Frideswide's twice on a Sunday, and the harmonium once at St Margaret's, earning 50p each time, so that he only had to find £1 a week for rent. He would cycle from Osney into town. The harmonium is still there. We look at it in the gloom. The church is very ancient, built on the site of an Anglo-Saxon church. The site was holy in pre-Reformation times because of its association with St Frideswide, the patron saint of Oxford, and the well beside the church had magical properties. Henry VIII visited it. From the twelfth century it came under the jurisdiction of the Priory of St Frideswide at Christ Church. I take on board these picturesque details because the place, with its healing well, its ancient churchyard, its unheated, unlit and numbingly cold nave under a tie-beam roof, all give – I imagine – a sense of what life was like in rural Oxford in medieval times. Inside the pulpit is an unpublicised and explicitly sensual carved relief of St Margaret, attributed to the caprine Eric Gill.

Outside is the famous well, immortalised by Charles Dodgson as the Treacle Well, and described by the Dormouse as the home of the three girls. (A treacle well was in fact a term for a healing well, treacle being a word for balm.) When Dodgson was asked by the vicar of the time what he should do with the well, he replied, 'Leave WELL alone.' After taking the cure, cripples would hang up their crutches in the church to demonstrate their new mobility. In the churchyard many generations of Pricketts are buried. In fact one of the Pricketts was Alice Liddell's nanny, and the model for the Red Queen. But here – in the bone-riddled ground – I see a grave, a more recent one, of Jan Laurens Van der Post, the son of Laurens Van der Post and the brother of Lucia Van der Post, the journalist. Van der Post worked with my father as a young journalist in Cape Town, and my father always regarded him as a fabulist, which J.D.F. Jones's recent biography seems to confirm. But by what route did the son end here in this churchyard? Before the war, Laurens had sent his family back to South Africa when he embarked on an affair with the woman who was eventually to become his second wife.

We walk back to Oxford. On the river an old college barge is moored, derelict. Even in my time at Oxford, many of the colleges still had barges moored on the Isis beyond Christ Church Meadow. They were in effect gentlemen's clubs, some lavishly equipped. The three or four that survive in private hands are scattered around the Thames now.

That night, after a reading at a bookshop, I walk around the Broad where a strange and wonderful display of fire in pots and braziers and chandeliers has been set up by a French group called Luminox. A band plays Brazilian music; great ropes hang from the Clarendon Building and the Sheldonian, supporting pots of fire. Broad Street and my old college appear to be engulfed in fire. It is an astonishing and stirring sight. I wonder if the organisers are aware that right here the Oxford martyrs, Cranmer, Ridley and Latimer, were burned at the stake in 1555. (They were, in fact, all Cambridge men.) The exact spot is commemorated in the Broad by a cobble cross.

Geza Vermes nominates as his favourite places some libraries that no longer exist and Bagley Wood on Boars Hill, owned by St John's College, which does. Geza and his wife Margaret have a delightful house, which backs on to the wood. Only members of the college and those five householders whose property adjoins the wood can use it. Geza has described it to me as an ideal place for meditation and thinking. It was a favourite haunt of Matthew Arnold's Scholar Gipsy:

> In autumn, on the skirts of Bagley Wood
> Where most the gipsies by the turf-edged way
> Pitch their smoked tents, and every bush
>   you see
> With scarlet patches tagg'd and shreds of grey,
> Above the forest-ground called Thessaly
> The blackbird, picking food,
> Sees thee, nor stops his meal, nor fears at all;
> So often has he known thee past him stray,
> Rapt, twirling in thy hand a wither'd spray,
> And waiting for the spark from heaven to fall.

After the dissolution of the monastic holdings, St John's was given the wood to provide the fellows with building timber and firewood. The whole wood is 550 acres, and is used for scientific studies of insects and birds and so on, as well as commercial logging; St John's has its own saw mill. The wood includes a large, untouched section dating back to the Middle Ages.

We set off on a walk; at one point almost every tree has a numbered bird box. Occasionally there are gaps that give views to farms and villages like Hinksey, which hint – like sketches that have been overpainted – at what Oxford must have been a hundred and fifty years ago, a series of palaces and temples set in a deeply rural countryside. Arnold loved these views of Oxford, and they must have been utterly magical. Bagley Wood is an astonishing place, just three miles from the centre of Oxford, but with a deep, undisturbed peace. Deer peer at us before ambling away – like Arnold's blackbird, not frightened, merely prudent. We don't see another person for an hour, but we rarely escape the susurration of the ring road.

Colin Lucas started slowly when I asked him for his favourite places, and then they poured out. Maybe when you live in Oxford you don't think of them in those terms until you are asked. His list included Balliol Garden Quad in moonlight, which he said was like looking across the Rhine at a minor principality when viewed from the steps of Hall; Turl Steet early on a summer morning; and Christ Church Meadow on a misty morning. His favourite objects included Powhatan's Mantle in the Ashmolean. He also liked Harris Manchester's Pre-Raphaelite stained glass, the Codrington Library in All Souls, small college gardens like that at Queen's, the doorway of the Octagon at Hertford College (once part of St Mary's church), the back gate to Christ Church, the staircase in the Radcliffe Camera and the fan-vaulted Divinity School.

Others recommended Wadham's gardens, St Edmund Hall Gardens, the Botanic Gardens, Holywell Cemetery, the Pitt-Rivers, the Norman Church of St Mary, Iffley, and endless nooks and crannies of various colleges, usually ones where they had been undergraduates. Duke Humfrey's Library was often remembered as was the Schools Quadrangle of the Bodleian. Specific parts of the river, Port Meadow and Wytham, and many villages within a short distance of Oxford also linger in the memory. I wonder again what it is about these gardens, quads and villages that so holds the imagination. Hugh Casson describes the 'squeeze points' that were part of the scheme of the colleges, deliberately designed so that after you have passed through a narrow entrance, you suddenly burst out into a quad, like the vast Tom Quad at Christ Church or the cloisters of New College. The quads give a sense of expectancy, of revelations and explorations to come. C.S. Lewis described the effect of entering his fictional college from the street:

The sense of gradual penetrations into a holy of holies was very strong. First you went through the Newton quadrangle which is dry and gravelly; florid but beautiful. Georgian buildings look down upon it. Next you must enter a cool tunnel-like passage, nearly dark at midday unless either the door into the hall should be open on your right or the buttery hatch to your left, giving you a glimpse of indoor daylight falling on panels, and a whiff of the smell of fresh bread. When you emerged from this tunnel you would find yourself in the medieval college: in the cloister of the much smaller quadrangle called Republic.

No undergraduate and probably very few of the permanent residents who stayed on has ever visited every quad and every garden in Oxford, but they all remember their own.

As I wandered round Oxford for the purposes of writing this book, I found myself surprised by how little of the topography I actually knew: quads and gardens and parks, churches and chapels had blurred in the imagination. And this too is part of the Oxford myth, that you imagine you know the place, but what you know is only those locations that relate directly to a particular period in your life, and one which is hopelessly coloured by the blitheness of lost youth. The more I have come to know about Adam von Trott, the more I find that his brief and ecstatic time in Oxford coloured the whole of his short subsequent life. His last letter to his mother before his execution in 1944 talks of his Oxford life as one of the twin axes of his existence.

I meet Helena Chance, a garden historian, to discuss Oxford gardens. She is an expert on their social effects and purposes. She says that these gardens were originally only for the use of the fellows, to allow them to recuperate and stimulate their intellects. Others provided fruit and fish, in the monastic tradition. Until the reforms of the nineteenth century, I have come to understand, the colleges were run largely for the benefit of the fellows, with the inconvenience of dealing with students avoided as far as possible. Some colleges had enormous holdings: Wadham has three gardens, and at one stage the college owned all the land to the north and possessed a market garden. Some of the Civil War ramparts are still there in the garden.

Helena Chance thinks that the Fellows' Private Garden at Corpus Christi is the most interesting in Oxford. David Leake, the gardener, believes in organic gardening. He doesn't rake up leaves, as they provide a home for insects, and he loves seedlings. Most garden writers love this garden, but a few think it is messy. (I thought it looked a little bosky when I visited.) She particularly loves David Leake's very traditional potting shed. Leake has the garden at its best in June, so that the students will not miss it. Helena also loves Wadham's private garden and the cemetery behind St Edmund Hall because it is one of the few spaces in Oxford undisturbed since the beginning, a fact attested by the presence of field mice in the garden. She tells me that when you look at sixteenth-century maps of Oxford, the changes that have taken place in the gardens, and the loss of gardens and spaces of all sorts, are almost numberless. The sense of tranquil history is hopelessly misleading.

Like Colin Lucas, she loves the Burne-Jones stained glass in Harris Manchester, and *Lazarus* by Epstein in New College chapel is another of her favourite things. But Magdalen, she suggests, is the ultimate in gardens, with ten gardeners, the deer park and the incomparable Addison's Walk, as well as a wonderful Fellows' Garden. And I would list this garden – estate might be a better word – as one of my favourite places in Oxford too. Helena believes that the gardens of Oxford should open less grudgingly to the public. The collegiate system is, after all, very convivial. Not only convivial, but a terrible loss for some when they go out into the real world.

9

It is almost Christmas. In the market an enormous wild boar and a deer hang in an improbably beautiful still life outside a butcher's shop. I am alone in Oxford. A huge Christmas tree stands in Broad Street, heeling in the wind. The lights on it are blue; for some reason they remind me of the bluebottles that used to end up on the beaches of Cape Town. I find I have an exact, and unnecessary, recall of physical facts of my childhood. There is another Christmas tree in Trinity's front quad, just beside the arch next to the chapel on the right and the fellows' dining room on the left. The lights on this tree are white. The President's lodgings are dark: Michael Beloff has left and the new man is expected soon. The presidential dog has been sighted, perhaps acting as a *vorlaufer*.

I have an eye infection; my eyes look like those of an albino rabbit. I wander the cold streets and every one of them summons a memory of some person, some incident and some girl. Here I remember meeting a girl from Lady Margaret Hall. She had told me I was the best-looking man in Oxford, palpably untrue, but still gratifying. I was dressed in my bullet-proof tweed suit with pink polo-neck. Later I discovered that a friend of mine was also seeing her. Perhaps he was the second-best-looking man in Oxford. We realised that we had sometimes spent consecutive nights in LMH; this suggested that there was some truth in the adage that there were enough girls in Oxford to go around if they went around fast enough. And here I remember stumbling from Exeter College after a mysterious, almost Masonic, evening with the Ambrosia Society, to which I had been elected although I never discovered by whom or for what purpose. The society served nothing but mead made by monks, and this may well have been its one and only meeting. It may even have been some sort of prank. The mead worked like novocaine on my face and I was unable to speak. And here, when I spent a few weeks in University College reworking my thesis, I met Bill Clinton. I wish I could say he made an impression on me, or better still, that I had made an impression on him, but neither is true. I only remember thinking that he had a good ole boy face. I walk down Longwall Street: here, outside Magdalen, where a Commemoration Ball was going on, I appeared with two friends in white coats, claiming to be from Black Boy Caterers, owned by the son of my landlady at that time, Mrs Stott. The coats came from the Moti Mahal, where I was a regular customer with my friend Salim Vahidi. We were shown into the college, but a security man asked why we were there and I said, 'We have come to carve the kedgeree,' which may have been alliterative, but somehow didn't strike the right note. 'Best fucking story I have heard all night,' said the security man, 'now fuck off.' So much for sixties deference.

Much later I walk to the coffee stall in St Giles and order a latte. The East European girl serving asks me if I am all right. I think she imagines that I may have been crying or that I am having a breakdown. Fine, I say, just tired; long flight from Canada. She clearly doesn't believe me. She says all right, as if to indicate that she understands that I want the subject closed. I am touched by her concern, but I find it a little worrying that I am giving an impression of loneliness. The truth is that behind the coney eyes I am very happy to be wandering the streets of Oxford alone. Every step of the way I find my mind vaulting, somewhat out of control. I find myself thinking of Mrs Stott and the letter I received not long ago from her older son Richard about his mother. I was an astonishingly anarchic and inconsiderate lodger. I had been thrown out with some others from lodgings in Chalfont Road after innumerable parties when finally I had gone too far by burning some of the furniture in the grate. (I am all too aware of how contemptible this sounds.) I was able to find new digs and Mrs Stott and I were brought together. She was from the North and was very proud of her three grown-up children, the one who was the caterer, Richard, then a tabloid journalist, later editor, twice, of the *Daily Mirror*, and Judith the actress, married to Dave Allen the Irish comic. I had a habit of losing my house keys and waking Mrs Stott up in the middle of the night, sometimes with some young woman, either timorous or drunken, in tow.

She said to me after a while, 'You are the worst gentleman I have had since Mr Zinoviev.'

It turned out that Mr Zinoviev had blown a hole in the ceiling with his twelve-bore shotgun. I detected that this event had, in retrospect, added glamour to Mrs Stott's life. I did my best to match Mr Zinoviev, but only on a relatively domestic scale, without the use of firearms. After a summer spent in Rome with Richard Burton's Oxford film of *Doctor Faustus*, I had an Italian lady friend, somewhat older than me, who used to ring the house phone at odd hours of the night. Mrs Stott was very interested in this relationship, and wanted to know exactly who she was. She would often answer the phone before I could get there, or she would leave me little notes about the gist of the emotional and mostly incoherent messages from the Eternal City. Mrs Stott had another house in Enstone, just to the north of Oxford, and she called this unremarkable place 'the gateway to the Cotswolds'. Sometimes she would remind me that she was related to the Pickford family, of long-distance removals fame. When I woke her during the night once too often, she told me that I would have to go in the morning. But in the morning she brought breakfast for two into my room, and pretended not to notice the human shape under the covers.

She was a wonderful woman and I was inordinately pleased to receive Richard Stott's letter, sent a year or so before he died, which suggested that she had liked me too and often spoke of me affectionately. Now I think, as the father of two grown-up boys, how cruel it was of me to have neglected my own mother, leaving South Africa at the age of twenty and never returning for any length of time, although in her last years, after my father died, I rang her almost every day. Mrs Stott, I now see, treated me as a wayward son. But even as I write this, I wonder how my mother really felt about my desertion, proud though she was of having an Oxford man for a son. I was thinking of her when I gave one of my characters in *White Lightning* the line about Oxford, that it was the Lourdes of Englishness.

Reading what I have just written about my escapades, I am struck by their *Charley's Aunt* quality. Not long ago I saw *Charley's Aunt* at the Oxford Playhouse. In the row in front of me were some mostly Chinese-American summer-school girls, who were trying to explain it, hopelessly, to each other. And it occurred to me as I watched that the idea put about by the English themselves, that Oxford was populated by idle upper-class buffoons, has lent to Oxford a ridiculously misleading and damaging image. But I see that I too was in thrall to the myth of Oxford as a louche and decadent place, although I think that even back in the sixties, when there really were some gormless peers wandering about, the whole *Brideshead* business was treated ironically. Recent undergraduates, including one of my sons, tell me that they and their friends were very aware of it and some even played up to it. But the truth is that Oxford has changed almost beyond recognition, if not outwardly, but in many significant ways. Noel Annan, in his book *The Dons*, claims that the Oxford of 1965 is as different from the Oxford of today as the Oxford of Jowett, but still it seems that the old habits of mind persist.

The light in Oxford on a winter's night is strangely friable. The wind has dropped and a mist has come in, as if it were just waiting its moment, so that the Christmas lights around the town are like the lights on the rigging of ships waiting to enter harbour and there are constellations of what could be talc around the lamps on the walls, producing a soft aureole. The gaps between buildings are being filled by this damp mist billowing determinedly in from the lowlands, and the whole aspect of Oxford has changed to something wonderfully beguiling, a dreamscape. A bicyclist in a dinner jacket goes by, followed by woman in a long dress, hoicked up. They vanish as suddenly as they came. Now a group of men and women, going to some do, which alcohol may make bearable, with other middle-aged people. They have that slightly goofy look that you often notice in academics, with their misguided attempts to look up to date, one man with a comedy bow tie, one woman with a jolly spangled dress. Another is wearing flashing earrings. Christmassy, I imagine her thinking, as she disappears, earrings winking, into the mist.

I am myself Christmassy, happy beyond belief, though my eyes are hurting, and I appear to be weeping.

ACKNOWLEDGEMENTS

Of the many people who have [illegible] [illegible], I would particularly like to [illegible] [illegible] Gardner [illegible] Wolfson College [illegible] and fellows of [illegible] [illegible] indebtedness to [illegible] [illegible] and colleagues [illegible] [illegible] truthfully say [illegible] [illegible] their kindness and [illegible]

[illegible] and [illegible] [illegible] to thank Liz Calder [illegible] contribute a book to her series [illegible] the City.

ACKNOWLEDGEMENTS

Of the many people who helped and advised me in Oxford, I would particularly like to thank Henry Hardy of Wolfson College, and the President and Fellows of Trinity College. A full list of my indebtedness to individuals, museums, libraries and colleges would be over-long, but I can truthfully say that I have encountered nothing but kindness and forbearance.

All at Bloomsbury are, I hope, aware of my affection and gratitude, but I would particularly like to thank Liz Calder, who invited me to contribute a book to her series 'The Writer and the City'.

A NOTE ON THE AUTHOR

Justin Cartwright is a graduate of Trinity College. His novels include the Booker shortlisted *In Every Face I Meet*, the acclaimed bestseller *The Promise of Happiness*, which won the Hawthornden Prize in 2005, *White Lightning*, which was shortlisted for the 2002 Whitbread Novel Award, and the 1998 Whitbread Novel Award winner *Leading the Cheers*. His most recent novel, *The Song Before It Is Sung*, was published in 2007. He was born in South Africa, and now lives in London.

A NOTE ON THE AUTHOR

Justin Cartwright is a graduate of Trinity College. His novels include the Booker-shortlisted *In Every Face I Meet*, the acclaimed bestseller *The Promise of Happiness*, which won the Hawthornden Prize in 2007, *White Lightning*, which was shortlisted for the 2002 Whitbread Novel Award, and the 1999 Whitbread Novel Award-winner *Leading the Cheers*. His most recent novel, *The Song Before It Is Sung*, was published in 2007. He was born in South Africa, and now lives in London.

A NOTE ON THE TYPE

The text of this book is set in Linotype Sabon, named after the type founder, Jacques Sabon. It was designed by Jan Tschichold and jointly developed by Linotype, Monotype and Stempel, in response to a need for a typeface to be available in identical form for mechanical hot metal composition and hand composition using foundry type. Tschichold based his design for Sabon roman on a fount engraved by Garamond, and Sabon italic on a fount by Granjon. It was first used in 1966 and has proved an enduring modern classic.

Binsey
Port Meadow
Woodstock Rd
Banbury Rd
Keble
St Giles
Ashmolean Museum
Martyrs' Me
Trini
Playhouse
Broa
Nuffield
George St
Oxford Union Society
Cornmarket
Sheldo
Covered Marke
St Aldate's
Chr Chu
Folly Br
ISIS
Bagley Wood
Boars Hill